Modeling the financial management of a commercial bank

Serge Moulin

Translated by Dr. Anne-Sophie Gintzburger

All rights reserved. In application of French law of the 11th of March 1957 (Article 41) and intellectual property law of the 1st of July, supplemented by law of the 3rd of January 1995, any partial or total copy of this publication for collective use is strictly forbidden without the express permission of the author. Every reproduction or use without the consent of the author is illegal.

© 2016 S. Moulin. ALM-VISION. All rights reserved.
ISBN 978-1-326-72835-9

ACKNOWLEDGMENTS

Asset Liability Management (ALM) issues are central to finance, whether they concern a bank, an institution, an SPV, a CLO, a defeasance structure... Indeed ALM is structurally related to the notion of banking leverage. Since the 2008 crisis, the entire profession is aware of how important it is to handle the subject in a way that is both thorough and accurate.

During my entire career and today still, my focus is to have our team provide in full transparency the highest quality service and scientific methodological support which are the only added values justifying our customers' trust. It has allowed us to build an open and confident dialogue with our customers. I always made sure that our experts could express their views and opinions entirely independently, because exchanging perspectives is the only way to progress.

ALM is a fundamental field. Yet it is complex, difficult and subtle because of the approximations required to remain efficient. It requires hard work, patience, consistency and clarity.

This book presents the concepts that led us to imagine the extraordinary tool that is ALM-Solutions® software. It is a condensed version of these strategic reflections, including major ALM themes that are best analyzed with a modern quantitative modeling approach.

This isn't an academic book. In many aspects, it simply introduces the reader to the field of Asset Liability Management. At times it does so from our perspective only. But globally, we are convinced that the book will contribute to nourish the thoughts of the readers and will invite them to exchange perspectives with us.

I would like to express once again my sincere thanks to our customers who have, in granting us their trust, gifted us with the motivation to continuously improve our services.

Serge Moulin
Founder & CEO, ALM-Vision

TABLE OF CONTENTS

ACKNOWLEDGMENTS.. 3

TABLE OF CONTENTS 5

ACRONYMS 9

INTRODUCTION 13

MODELING A BANK 17

Guiding principles of modeling 17
   Globality 17
   Unicity 20
   Accounting as a benchmark 21
   Pragmatism 23
   Taking care of the data warehouse 23
   Transparency 25

Credits 25
   Credit-by-credit approach or approach by homogeneous class? 25
   Prepayments: modeling and pricing 27
   Modeling 28
   Theoretical optimum prepayment 33
   Aggregated behaviors 34
   Pricing 36
   Regarding new production 39
   Assets and liabilities in currencies 47

Deposits of undefined maturity 48

Other balance sheet items 54

Securities and off-balance sheet items 54
Fixed assets, intangible assets, tax assets 57

Static or dynamic gaps **58**
Reconciling dynamic and static gap analysis 59
A simple scenario 60
Which duration for financial management steering policy? 71

Liquidity analysis **72**
About liquidity transformation and targets of runoff 75
Bank liquidity leverage 76

Taking accounting into consideration **82**

The connections between different types of risk **83**
Scenarios to consider 83
Ratios or crisis scenarios: two complementary methods 90
Simulations with discretionary or stochastic scenarios? 91
What sort of liquidity transformation should one accept? 92

Financial management analysis **92**
Defining analytical activities 92
Internal rates and reinvestment conventions 97
Internal rates in practice 102
Rate and volume effect 103
Valuation of deposit collection and loans 104
Limits of the analysis 107

REGULATIONS 109

Interest rate risk **110**
The July 2004 Basel text 110
The standard method for calculating interest rate risk 112

Basel III and banking leverage **114**
Recalling Basel regulations 115

Covered Bonds 126
Securitization 126
Calculating profitability net of risk 128

Basel III and liquidity monitoring 130

Regulatory ratios and indicators 132

BALANCE SHEET MANAGEMENT 135

Funding policies 135
Available market tools 135
What tool, for which purpose, and to what extent? 139
Steering through customer business 140

Managing capital surplus 141

Related financial and commercial activities 143

Bank bail-outs 143
Three phases of a bail-out 144
Defeasance structures 149
Guarantees 151

The banker's traps 153

CONCLUSION: MAINTAIN LONG-TERM VISION 160

BIBLIOGRAPHY 163

ACRONYMS

ABCP	:	Asset-Backed Commercial Paper Programs
ABS	:	Asset-Backed Securities
ALM	:	Asset and Liabilities Management
B&S	:	Black and Scholes
bn	:	billion
CC	:	Consumption of Core Capital
CCF	:	Credit Conversion Factor
CAD	:	Capital Adequacy Directive
CAPM	:	Capital Asset Pricing Model
CDO	:	Collateralized Debt Obligation
CDR	:	Constant Default Rate
CDS	:	Credit Default Swap
CET1	:	Common Equity Tier I
CF	:	Commodities Finance
CIB	:	Corporate and investment banking
CMS	:	Constant Maturity Swap
CP	:	Commercial Paper
CR	:	Customer Rate
CRD	:	Capital Ration Definition
CSR	:	Community Solvency Ratio
DDM	:	Dividend Discount Model
DTA	:	Deferred tax assets
DTL	:	Deferred tax liabilities
E3M	:	Euribor 3 Months
EAD	:	Exposures At Default
ECB	:	European Central Bank
EIB	:	European Investment Bank
EL	:	Expected Loss
ELA	:	Emergency Liquidity Assistance
ESR	:	European solvency ratio
GGCP	:	Government Guaranteed Commercial Paper

HJM	:	Heath Jarrow Morton
HQLA	:	High Quality Liquidity Assets
HVCRE	:	High Volatility Commercial Real-Estate
IFRS	:	International Financial Reporting Standards
IMF	:	International Monetary Fund
IPRE	:	Income Producing Real-Estate
IRB	:	Internal Ratings Based approach
IRC	:	Internal Rate of Cession
L&R	:	Loans & Receivables
LCR	:	Liquidity Coverage Ratio
LGD	:	Loss Given Default
LTRO	:	Long-Term Refinancing Operations
LVaR	:	Liquidity Value Adjusted at Risk
M	:	Maturity
M1	:	Money supply
MDB	:	Multilateral Development Banks
mn	:	million
MtM	:	Mark to Market
NBI	:	Net Banking Income
NIM	:	Net Interest Margin
NPL	:	Non Performing Loans
NSFR	:	Net Stable Funding Ratio
OCI	:	Other Comprehensive Income
OF	:	Object Finance
OTC	:	Over The Counter
P/BV	:	Price to Book Value
PD	:	Probability of Default
PER	:	Price Earning Ratio
PF	:	Project Finance
PPP	:	Public Private Partnership
REPO	:	Repurchase agreement and sell/buy-back
RMBS	:	Residential Mortgage Backed Securities

ROA	:	Return on Assets
ROE	:	Return on Equity
RSE	:	European Solvency Ratio (*Ratio de Solvabilité Européen*)
RW	:	Risk Weight
RWA	:	Risk Weighted Assets
SL	:	Specialized Lending
SME	:	Small and Medium-sized Enterprises
SPE	:	Special Purpose Entity
SCR	:	Solvency Capital Ratio
T1	:	Tier 1
UCITS	:	Undertakings for Collective Investment in Transferable Securities
UL	:	Unexpected Loss
VaR	:	Value-at-Risk
VIF	:	Value in Force

INTRODUCTION

The purpose of a commercial bank is to provide services to clients, to provide means of payment and cash management tools, to safeguard client assets, to assist clients with investments and give them access to credit facilities. Such services are beneficial to the entire community and require significant resources, particularly capital funds. The financial compensation for providing these services is consequently proportional to risk incurred. Due to its key economic role in providing leverage and financing to the domestic market, the banking sector is strictly regulated by financial authorities.

This definition of the banking profession, though trivial in appearance, contains the foundations guiding key decisions in the industry. The banking profession is primarily the result of a thought process, of a reflection derived from the systematic analysis of the global economy juxtaposed to the financial situation of each client. Such strategic and tactical positioning guides decisions underlying the development of different banking activities. It translates into the way that the bank is managed given that a banker is both a leading business executive (head of a company) and a merchant. Yet unlike what is characteristic of other trades, the banker's core commodity is money. Looked at from this perspective and even more with the dematerialization of transactions, a bank is in essence a balance sheet.

Just as an industrial actor would see its core business best represented by its factories, the equivalent of a factory to a bank is its balance sheet. To use the words of Liszt, a balance sheet to a banker is what a piano is to a concert pianist. It should be central to all his or her concerns. Yet a balance sheet evolves, gets distorted, transformed, increases, sometime shrinks under the pressures of the economic environment and decisions from bank management. Most of the movements are gradual. With the exception of bankruptcy induced by crises that can literally disintegrate a balance sheet in a matter of hours, it is as difficult to alter the risk profile of a bank as to steer a cargo ship. Most new implementations manifest in results only gradually. In the case of a commercial bank, such gradual changes are to be desired. In fact, one of the leading indicators of risk in a bank's life cycle is growth that is excessively rapid. From the Crédit Lyonnais scandal to the 2008 crisis, this appears to be an absolute rule. Whereas a balance sheet grows steadily, it can be destroyed in a matter of hours. Bear Stearns believed that it could survive at 4:00 p.m. NYT, yet at 4:30 p.m., after the withdrawal of an amount close to USD 20 bn. dollars by two clients, the bank was brought to the ground, surviving on what could be likened to a morphine pump administered by the Federal Reserve of New York via J. P. Morgan.

Bank balance sheets are a mirror of the economy. They contain the essence of the great crises: from the excessive leverage in Japan or in 1929 to the excessive leverage which again gave rise to the 2008 crisis... The disintermediation trend in this sense does not resolve the intrinsic risk in credit leverage. It just transfers it to other economic actors, ones that are often less able to manage it. Disintermediation did not enable the USA to power through the subprime crisis, in fact it contributed to aggravating the situation by spreading the damage into the balance sheets of a large number of banking institutions heavily exposed to subprime loans and often too weak to absorb the impact of such loss.

Given these elements, it is surprising that banks do not have much in terms of long-term management tools for their balance sheet. General management rarely seems interested in this complex and technical matter. What tends to happen is that the matter is delegated to specialists, supplying little in the way of means and accepting methodologies without discussing the best suited strategy for the unique situation faced by the institution. Many ALM committees are paralyzed by formalities and suffer from insufficient resources given their regulatory duties; too many budgets are enacted for one year only, or for a maximum of three years, in an inflexible manner that evades taking into consideration different potential economic scenarios faced by the institution. Regulators themselves may be embroiled in this rigid approach unless they encourage banking institutions to upgrade, to restructure, and to reflect on their actions and on the management of their institutions. A balance sheet is a unified whole. It expresses the overall risks faced by the bank: interest rate risk, credit risk, liquidity risk, management cost risks, foreign exchange risk...

Understanding and simulating the balance sheet is a method that banks use to manage their budget, to decide on their transformation strategy, to measure interest rate risk, and test their ability to absorb shocks in the event of a systemic crisis ... Nowadays, in too many institutions, these different areas are treated separately, and often with so many hypotheses and conventions that people tend to get lost in the process. Yet new technologies and substantial advances in computing power and information systems facilitates accurate management of ALM processes. This book offers a contemporary approach that takes into account these new parameters and that is as thorough as possible in its methodology given the subject matter. It is based on certain enduring principles:

- Reality: sticking as tightly to reality as possible.

- Transparency: approximations despite their necessity for the sake of efficiency must be justified.

- Practicality: to remain both practical and operational.

These three principles consist somewhat of a breakthrough in the methods based on static balance sheets to which a great number of arbitrary conventions apply. Yet these older methods can be reconciled with real life scenarios. This breakthrough, rather than a rejection of one of the first effective management method, should rather be seen for what it is. It is simply a cutting-edge new direction in efficient banking management. Nor should it be interpreted as a break from the regulatory guidelines: quite the contrary in fact since it is based on the valuable reflections and recommendations of the Basel Committee.

The committee's guidelines are fundamental in terms of banking management. They should not be seen as a series of constraints in the negative sense of the term or of useless recommendations but rather they should be taken as a valuable source of considerations, of areas of improvement and of recommendations that go beyond rules and ratios. In fact the committee highlights regularly that these are to be considered as minimum requirements, conscious of the real conditions faced by many banks. The Basel II text, pillar 2, *Principles for the management and supervision of interest rate risk* (July 2004) and the Basel III text are the obligatory fundamentals for developing a modern, sound and robust approach to the financial management of a banking institution.

The book was published to formalise the methodology at the core of the creation of our ALM-Solutions® software. This constitutes a supplementary theoretical and methodological support in addition to our existing online assistance. It contains the basis of the banking viewpoint that has brought us to effectuate the numerous necessary choices involved in the creation of this powerful management tool. ALM-Solutions® does however go beyond the perspective that we present. Like other software packages, its results can be interpreted and used in a number of ways. In fact we have experienced this every day. With every client our interpretation is enriched with a new angle, a new perspective, a particular way of seeing an asset, or imagining a crisis scenario and of its repercussions on the balance sheet... This book often offers a choice of interpretation relative to ALM-Solutions® which is that of the author. The reader may see other angles. The ALM-Solutions® team is in fact always interested in the idea of modifying their approach in the interest of improving results: we are primarily at the service of our clients' needs and vision. This book is therefore more a means of sharing the journey of our thoughts and reasoning to the reader relating to the major challenges that they are confronted with in order to engage in a dialogue from a formal methodological basis.

It also consists of a synopsis of the major areas in ALM management and will be useful to anyone in management control, ALM management, financial administration or someone seeking a perspective of this sector in its globality.

It goes beyond this as well, as I have added some thoughts on people and recent events in the financial sector. The final reflection that I refer to here is for intellectual stimulation, it is a testimonial with indirect connections to the formal and austere topic of ALM. In truth, I hesitated for a while to keep these thoughts in the book. In Europe it is common to keep technical work separate from reflections on human behavior. Such reflections by their nature, are more delicate. I decided to keep them in the book because beyond what we observe on the technical side, there are people. It is people who make decisions and choices on the tactical and strategic direction of the banking institution. Under certain conditions, such choices can have irrecoverable consequences for a bank. This last part of the book offers the reader an opportunity to meditate on the banking sector, on human nature and on the behavior of those who work in it.

MODELING A BANK

Steering a bank is a long-term process for which a banker must always anticipate. The essence of the banking business is to bet on the future, the future success of an industrial project, the future ability of a client to make timely repayments, future market movements, future interest rates, the future economic environment... in many ways it is a bet on the manner in which the financial institution's balance sheet and income statement will react to future fluctuations. It is therefore vital to understand how a bank's balance sheet will react to an economic scenario that will most likely impact several of its items. It is one of the major tasks entrusted to financial and general management[1].

At the operational level, a number of banking departments are involved in the process. Three departments are involved in a major way:

- The financial department and its ALM modeling teams managing interest rate risk and liquidity risk. Their projections are of use to refinancing teams, to treasury and potentially to the strategy department.

- Financial management teams work on previsions and steering the company's financial results.

- Risk management teams model and control balance sheet risk.

These teams assist management in steering financial and client activity. To succeed in modeling one's bank, an achievement that only few banks have successfully completed, management must base its decisions on key principles that are found in the Basel text.

Guiding principles of modeling

Globality

The first stage of modeling is to understand the balance sheet to then simulate its reactions to certain events. To get to this stage, the most

---

[1] Basel Committee, principles for the management and supervision of interest rate risk, July 2004, principles 1, 2 and 6 "It is essential that banks have interest rate risk measurement systems that capture all material sources of IR risk and that assess the effect of IR changes..."

important item in a commercial bank, the credit portfolio, must be modeled together with other balance sheet items. The primary and most common error is to process only part of the balance sheet with the excuse that the rest will not change or that it is managed separately. Many errors stem from this assumption. Real instances:

- disregarding the effect of rates on an inflation swap portfolio
- disregarding the effect of rates on an investment portfolio
- the non-consolidation of risk between a bond portfolio and a credit activity under the same name
- disregarding the impact of a change in the economic environment on a subsidiary or an activity
- disregarding the link between credit spreads, liquidity, the closing of the market, a decrease in rates, an increase in loss
- poorly understood sensitivity of some fees to rates
- disregarding the connection between credit fees and volume.

It is therefore crucial that each item is integrated to the model. This includes fees and charges. There is one other reason for this overall approach that we term 'Globality': the reconciliation of the accounts. Adopting a global approach is in fact the only way to ensure that we are truly representing the entire bank and have not left out an element that will be later found to be crucial to our model. Management is generally only aware of the balance sheet and the comprehensive income statement. In order to adequately respond to questions that management may have, the overall activities need to be comprehensively integrated into the model. The regulator adopts the same stance as the one highlighted in the July 2004 Basel text[2].

Screenshot 1: Screenshot of a balance sheet: all items must be included

---

[2] § 19 page 6 "...even traditional sources of non-interest income such as transaction processing fees are becoming more IR sensitive..", principle 6 page 14 § 42 "As a general rule, it is desirable for any measurement system to incorporate IR risk exposures arising from the full scope of bank's activities..." and appendix 1 § 7 p28 "... most gap analyses fail to capture variability in non-interest revenue and expenses, a potential important source of risk to current income".

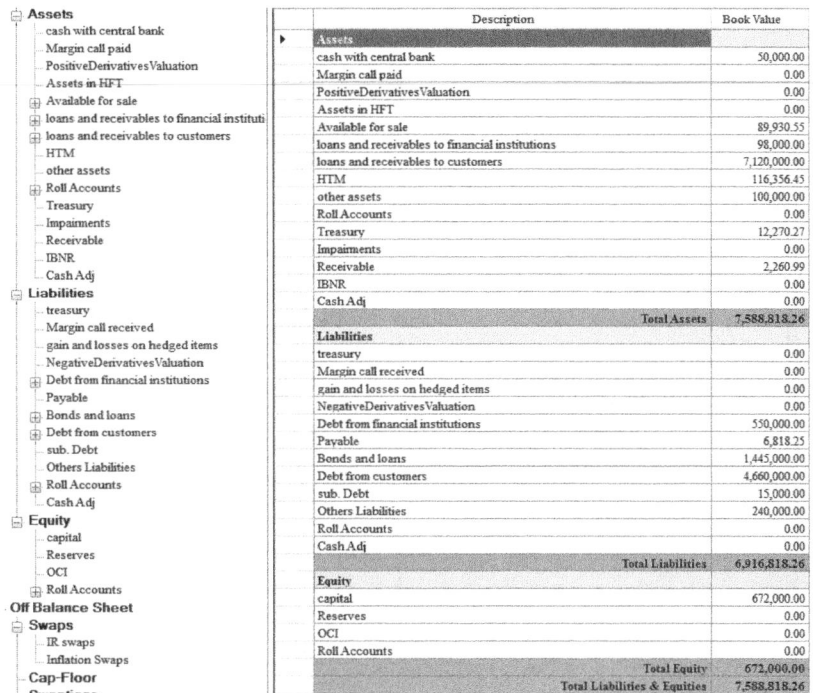

Globality therefore also signifies modeling both the balance sheet AND the income statements. This is actually the best way to get a sense of the quality of a model. Impact that may seem relatively trivial for the balance sheet can be far more impactful on the income statement.

Screenshot 2: Modeling example: the entire income statement is modeled

Result

	Opening Balan...	11/2013 - 10/2...	11/2014 - 10/2...	11/2015 - 10/2...
Book Values - Assets	7,588,818.26	7,710,061.2	7,822,207.17	7,931,185.19
Book Values - Liabilities ...	7,588,818.26	7,710,061.2	7,822,207.17	7,931,185.19
Book Values - Liabilit...	6,916,818.26	6,984,929.75	7,057,901.73	7,120,849.71
Book Values - Equity	672,000	725,131.45	764,305.43	810,335.48
Interest Income - Assets		239,416.36	239,810.51	259,594.93
Interest Expenses - Liabil...		86,545.91	87,097.48	95,633.22
Net Interest Income		152,870.46	152,713.04	163,961.71
Gain/Losses on Financial...				
Commissions & Others		97,560	100,440	103,320
Net Banking Income		250,430.46	253,153.04	267,281.71
Cost		-144,780	-146,770	-149,640
Income before impairmen...		105,650.46	106,383.04	117,641.71
Impairment Charge		-20,855.75	-21,652.34	-22,337.85
Income Pre Tax		84,794.7	84,730.69	95,303.86
Income tax benefit / (expe...		-28,830.2	-28,808.43	-32,403.31
Net Income		55,964.5	55,922.26	62,900.55
Dividends		2,833.05	16,748.27	16,870.5
ROE		7.72 %	7.33 %	7.78 %
Cost/Income Ratio		57.81 %	57.98 %	55.99 %
Periodic ROA		0.73 %	0.71 %	0.79 %
Yield - Assets		3.13	3.09	3.3
Yield - Liabilities & Equit...		1.24	1.24	1.35
RWA	4,482,500	4,536,460.06	4,606,104.11	4,800,260.81
Core Equity	672,000	725,131.45	764,305.43	810,335.48
Tiers 1	672,000	725,131.45	764,305.43	810,335.48
Regulatory Capital	672,000	725,131.45	764,305.43	810,335.48
Solvency Ratio on Core E...	14.99 %	15.98 %	16.59 %	16.88 %

Unicity

The second principle is unicity. Given the complexity of the subject and the work required to simulate a bank as well as the importance of efficient coordination between different teams, a global modeling tool is a strategic advantage at the financial and operational levels. Financially, the savings are major: a dedicated tool that is fed data in an automated fashion results in valuable savings in terms of staff numbers involved and time costs. More importantly, a quality tool reduces redundant coverage. It also reduces the occurence of contradictory decisions, from the piling up of errors due to poor coordination, to the misunderstanding of phenomena or errors of appreciation that are inevitable when only partial calculations are completed, often in a context of emergency and while lacking adequate tools. Only a clean and global tool that allows for modeling over the duration of at least an entire economic cycle or, if the bank has a long-term accounting structure, up to at least 80% of the renewal of the credit portfolio, gives the necessary vision required for the strategic reflection of management on client activity, liquidity and on the reinvestment of its own funds. The latter are, as we will see, key elements not only to the survival of the institution but also to its profitability.

Accounting as a benchmark

The third principle is to respect financial reporting norms. As an external reference, accounting figures are the ones that are closely looked at by shareholders and by management. Accrual accounting and cash accounting work according to guidelines that are constantly debated but that adapt well on the whole to long-term business. Deviations from the accounting guidelines result in two types of risk. The first risk is that of losing credibility and communication strength when interacting with management and shareholders. The second is the risk of measuring inaccurately the timing of the impact of movements on the bank. Cash accounting has limits that were highlighted once again during the 2008 crisis; revaluing one's own debt mark to market provides exceptional results despite the bank approaching default. Regarding assets, it would be both disastrous and absurd to revaluate credit using spreads deducted from extrapolations on different markets that became illiquid due to panic. In fact there is always a difference between the quoted market value of a liquid asset exchanged in reasonable amounts and its total value, or the entire price that a potential buyer is willing to pay. This is why IPOs are never made at market value. The difference in price can be explained with the use of a control value or something akin to the potential synergy that the buyer considers to be gaining, plus revenue increase and cost reduction. The truth of the matter is that for the majority of assets there is no actual market price, there are merely guidelines that bring some balance to the notion of mark to market. MtM is actually useful only in the case of specific market activities. To conclude, a bank is a brand with clients, fees, employees… Methodology for net asset valuation that does not take into account ongoing banking operations, the continuous regeneration of the balance sheet as well as the bank's economic and social role is therefore simply abstract and most often inapplicable.

The present value of the impact of interest rate movements on future banking income provides an estimate of the impact on capital funds that we believe to be more pertinent than the market value difference of each line. We believe this to be the case because the present value of spreads depends, as observed during the crisis, on the volumes phenomena (supply and demand) of the markets and that they differ, sometimes quite considerably, from their balance value (connected to PD[3] and LGD[4]). Proof of this is the increase in spreads in the range of 800 bp to 1,000 bp on papers that were redeemed at par without significant increase in risk on the lower tranches.

To summarize, accounting provides the official incomes statement, a snapshot that is the basis of decisions by shareholders, analysts and regulators. Yet it is the balance sheet that provides a realistic image of the actual standing of treasury. Modeling should therefore stick as tightly as possible to accounting guidelines, not only for reasons of pragmatic management but also because within the choice of false perspectives of the bank's situation, it remains, to quote Churchill, 'the best of the worst systems'. The price at which the bank's assets are exchanged on the market provides only an indication of the real value of the potential future incomes in a particular configuration of the economy and of the risk premium required by investors.

Having said that, modeling the bank requires more detailed data than can be found in the accountancy chain with market indications, client segments, product types… When extracting this data from the source, we find differences with the accounting statements. ALM is not an exact science and a margin of error relative to accounting is tolerated (experience indicates that a 1% error on the balance sheet is a perfectly negligible error). One must simply evaluate on a continual basis this margin of error to ensure that it does not amplify, which is fairly easy to assess given that the balance sheet will easily and rapidly display absurd figures if it amplifies.

---

[3] PD (Probability of Default): default probability of the debtor.
[4] LGD (Loss Given Default): loss in the event of default, taking into account any possible recovery and collateral.

Pragmatism

The last principle embodies pragmatism and patience: an essential operating rule for a banker who needs to project the impact of management decisions over the long-term. An item can be at first subject to approximate modeling. What matters is that it be structured in such a manner that teams can continue to progress while improving the model over time without modifying its global architecture. This constraint that seems rather logical provides a structuring framework for the model. To model simple assets such as a series of cash flows can fast become extremely complex if different norms relating to dates, rates, spreads, delayed starts...etc. are not taken into account. All models should be built on structures that are generic enough so that they can be completed without having to modify the core of the system.

Pragmatism is particularly reflected by the choice in the level of accuracy. The accuracy level that is necessary to complete the model will vary depending on the items. Some items such as fixed assets may be easily represented by a single line. Others may need to be modeled line by line, as is the case for many portfolio assets (especially if some of them are structured assets). The rule is to back the decision of chosing one model over another so that it may be revised at a later stage because business activity levels can vary over time. Loans in an emerging economy with margins of 8% and unpredictible risk do not require the same modeling accuracy as German mortgages with margins of 10 cents.

Pragmatism has another function: it keeps team focus on targets that are useful to the business. Financial management control can naturally lead to carrying out analysis, even if only for peace of mind. Seeking reassurance through analysis is however a tangent from the core objectives of financial management which is to facilitate service improvement and bank profitability through assessments and quantified analysis of its business.

Taking care of the data warehouse

The secret to a successful and useful model lies in the source database. Data warehouses should be under the attentive care of management. Far from just being 'the plumbing' as we so often hear it referred to, their structuring function in financial institutions is crucial especially given the growing number if regulatory constraints. Their architecture and maintenance is strategic. This of course requires complete and extensive documentation for each input database, and especially that of the core one, the credit chain.

Most banks have data warehouses that enable assembling their production databases for management purposes: calculating regulatory ratios, LCR, financial analysis ... ALM does not generally require the creation of additionnal databases but rather an accurate use of the existing ones.

The difficulty lies especially in the great variety of data sources with, generally speaking, at least six basic sources of data:

Figure 1

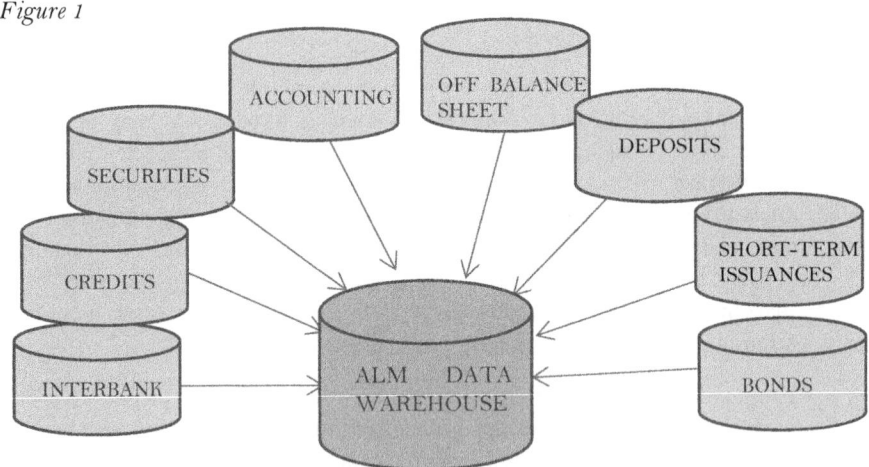

We will examine more in detail how to simplify the process of gathering the required inputs. The key point is that in general the information is already available. If it isn't, it is necessary that it should be placed into the institution's warehouses, independently of the ALM modeling. Yet recreating these connections with the motive that one should have access to more valid data is a classic error that can prove to be very expensive, not only financially but also in terms of hours of work by the team. The result is also generally heavier, making the data warehouses storage redundant and leads to pointless doubling of maintenance work.

Transparency

Intellectual integrity and honesty is fundamental to all financial management. In ALM banking, the great danger is the 'black box'[5] approach that hides major errors or purely speculative positions under a technical pseudo jargon. Transparency is the only way to improve and stabilize the processes that secure complex projects. It also leads to avoiding the severe mistakes that led to the failure of savings & loans (USD 120b. loss in the 1980s) or to the false credit hedges from JP Morgan in 2012 that damaged the reputation of the banking profession. Transparency is a regulatory requirement that is echoed throughout the Basel texts[6]. Transparency makes it possible to have reasonable and justifiable approximations and leads to considerable improvement of work over time.

Credits

The most important item in a bank's balance sheet is also the one for which there is the most experience in terms of modeling due to the securities market. Nearly all types of loans have been securitized in the past and therefore needed to be modeled: prime mortgages, sub-primes, alt-A, retail or office CMBS, CLO, commercial credit, project or asset financing, consumer credit, restructured credit, TRUPS, LBO... Each class leads to a specific approach even if there are general rules, the most important being the application of the law of large numbers.

Credit-by-credit approach or approach by homogeneous class?

The god of statistics has no pity and never deviates from his laws. A uniform credit portfolio with homogeneous technical characteristics (rate, duration, nominals, amortizing types, guarantees...) and borrower characteristics (profile, reason for credit...) can be perfectly modeled by class, as is the case for mortgage loans. Recalculating credit amortization, credit by credit, is most often pointless because in this case the improvement that we get in the degree of accuracy turns out to be negligible compared to the two major

---

[5] Basel committee, principles for the management and supervision of interest rate risk, July 2004, page 15-16 § 51 "techniques using sophisticated simulations should be used carefully so that they do not become "black boxes" producing numbers that have the appearance of precision..."

[6] Basel committee, principles for the management and supervision of interest rate risk, July 2004, principle 10 "regular independent reviews and evaluations of the effectiveness of the system..."

hazards of anticipated repayment rate and default rate. This method takes too much time for the calculation and does not add any real accuracy.

The annual amortization on a loans portfolio of linear depreciation spread over a 4 to 14 years depreciation period is 11.68%. By modeling this portfolio on one single line of duration corresponding to the rounding up of the closest month to the 'average life', that is to say 103 months, we obtain a linear amortization of 11.65% per year. The estimation error is of 0.3%. It is truly random in the sense that rounding up can be higher or lower.

This modeling error is clearly negligible when compared to error on the prepayment rate that can quickly reach 2 or even 3 points and is not risk free in its impact over the entire portfolio.

Table 1: estimation error

Duration Month	Year	Qty.	Annual amort.	Avg. life
60	5	1	0.200	2.00
72	6	1	0.167	2.50
84	7	1	0.143	3.00
96	8	1	0.125	3.50
108	9	1	0.111	4.00
120	10	1	0.100	4.50
132	11	1	0.091	5.00
144	12	1	0.083	5.50
156	13	1	0.077	6.00
168	14	1	0.071	6.50
180	15	0	0.000	7.00
Total		10	1.168	3.78
103	8.58	10	1.165	3.79
Error			-0.3%	

If one adds to that the risk of new business production (assets, profit margin), to then go through the calculations loan by loan becomes counterproductive as by using this method we lose the rapidity and flexibility necessary for the model to guide operational decisions.

This point is a fundamental one. The costs of implementing a bank balance sheet simulation is not proportional: a simple tool using reasonable approximations will have relatively minor implementation costs for a classic entity – less than EUR 100,000 in the simplest cases and up to several hundreds of thousands for more complex structures[7] – whereas a tool that tries to reproduce the entirety of the balance sheet's key elements (credits and assets), line by line, will cost several million or even tens of millions of Euros. And, in the latter case, the results often differ to what was expected. As it is too heavy to manipulate and particularly to maintain, the tool rapidly becomes abstract and unusable for its primary objective which is aiding in steering the bank. It is therefore confined to regulatory work, providing a resemblance of precision, until the regulator requires an audit at which point the omissions in the supply, or the methodological errors buried in its complexity, are discovered.

However, the larger loans often have highly different characteristics. This requires that they be modelled line by line: it is true for borrower's profiles, judicial clauses or even the types of guarantee concerned.

The bank already de facto differentiates between these loans in the liquidity ratio calculations, as Basel III for example accepts the treatment of real estate loans to individuals in a general class whereas it requires the default probabilities loan by loan for the activities of large businesses. The ALM model therefore only builds on the methodology used for the calculation of the solvency ratio. It is actually logical in a global approach; the tool used for a banking balance sheet model should in fact also enable the simulation of the liquidity ratio as well as the cost of risk. The two requirements, risk and ALM, actually share the same data source for the loans and assets which justifies a joint data warehouse from the perspective of the IT architecture.

Prepayments: modeling and pricing

Prepayments led to a great amount of publications due to the development of RMBS. The risk is well known. They are loan renegotiations and anticipated prepayments decided by the clients following a lowering in the interest rates and effected without penalty (or with a lower penalty to that of the market value variation). In the case of a lowering of interest rates, the prepayments evidently induce a lack of earnings or even bring about a clear loss, particularly in the case of market refinancing.

---

[7] Depending on the consultants work and their methodological approach, we assume that the data are available in a data warehouse

Of course, banks are aware of the phenomenon that can amplify in size in the case of a major movement in interest rates. But they are still having difficulties in modeling it and evaluating it as the phenomenon can have massive consequences in terms of cash flow (see graphic below) and the sensitivity of the portfolio (see following graphic).

Graph 1: Cash flows generated by a loan pool with constant annuity of an initial duration of 12 years.

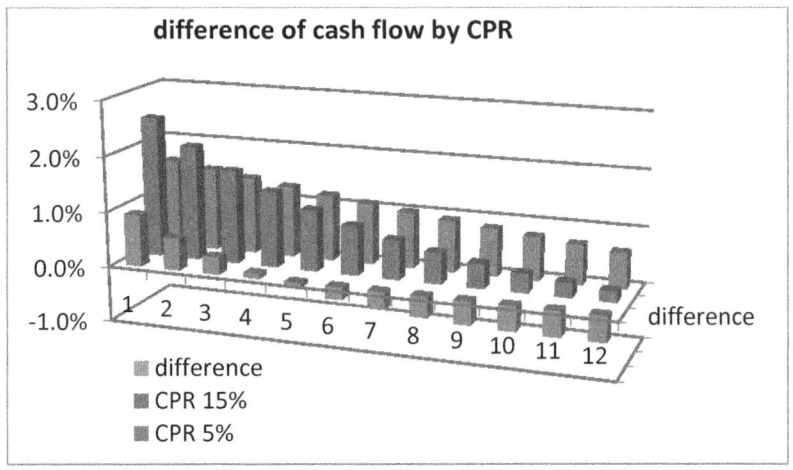

Modeling

The prepayment or renegotiation behavior modeling is the most important and delicate phase. We can distinguish two types of repurchases:

• The structural prepayments are independent of the interest rates or economic cycle: This is often related to decisions linked to life events, revenue income, divorces, deaths, accidents, births (purchase of a larger house), children leaving home... These events are mostly independent of the economic cycle. They are easy to take into account as they reduce the true duration of a loan pool. Depending on the markets, this phenomenon can convey between 3% to 10% to the remaining nominal each year. It is therefore a key phenomenon and error in its estimation will have a greater impact than, for example, calculation errors in the cash flow of a pool of credits on a market over a quarter for an initial duration of 8 to 12 years.

Graph 2: Modified duration according to anticipated prepayments (initial duration 12 years)

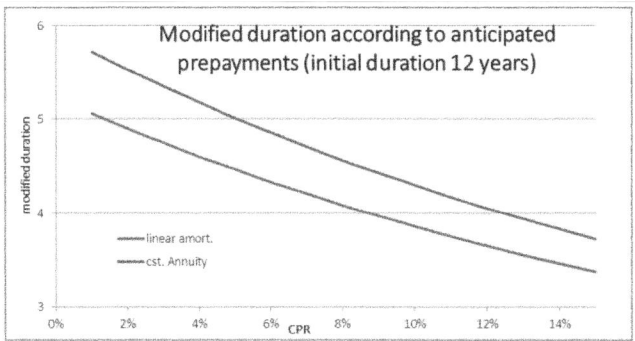

- The prepayments linked to the economic cycle, and particularly the interest rates: during a period of decrease in rates, if the client does not pay a penalty on the market price, their best decision is to exercise their option and repay in anticipation, ready to contract a new loan. A decrease in rates is often in fact linked to a recession situation therefore an increase in the claims that generate losses in credit but also loss in terms of interest rates. Inversely, during a period of increase in rates, clients that have the opportunity to repay by anticipation (due to an unexpected cash income for example) would be best to keep their loan and invest their funds. The rate of anticipated repayments is therefore lowered.

The factors that influence the prepayment rate of a client traditionally are:

- The market value of the difference in rates with the new market conditions (the rate difference multiplied by the sensitivity): This is the most important factor. However, one can observe that customers are more sensitive to the variation of rate (independently from the modified duration) than the MtM as it is difficult for them to estimate MtM.

- The credit size: clients with a higher income tend to take larger loans and, more often, and more efficiently, perform a rate comparison and decide on arbitrating the bank. Prepayment can generate fixed costs (on the guarantees for example) or even hidden costs (even if it's just the time taken for the operation) which are proportionately less. Regarding real estate, credits lower than €100,000 that are repaid in anticipation occur half as much as credits of €200,000 or more.

- The threshold effect known as 'Media effect': Borrowers have a higher tendency to renegotiate their credits when the rates approach historic lows. The intensity of the wave repurchasing is also greater if the lower threshold is older and is mentioned in the media.

- The credit spread: The larger the original spread, the weaker the probability for renegotiation. This is linked to client characteristic: more risky, more loyal, less sensitive to price...

On the real estate market (the most important market for retail banks), other specific factors enter into consideration:

- Real Estate prices affect transaction volumes and market activity relating to mortgage loans. A rising market promotes transactions, often leading to a period of growth and increased anticipated prepayments (independently of interest rates). Note that real estate prices can also, as was the case with the sub-primes, have a direct impact on the claims, and does so even more than the credit provided on the basis of collateral based on the borrower's financial position.

- The economic environment: a growing economy promotes mobility and the enrichment of its citizens as well as their trust in the future and therefore their credit decisions (but it can also promote inflation that encourages a reverse effect).

- Seasonality is important too with a number of major transactions in the spring, before the end of the school year, that therefore shows a statistical rate of prepayment 2 to 3 points higher than average.

Formally, customers are the owner of an American option to cancel a swap (if one neglects the spread effect). In theory, if they were rational, they would exercise the day where the intrinsic value is superior to the value of keeping the option. This time can be easily modeled in a simple Cox-Ross tree model. In reality, customers are not rational professional traders with real time quotes available. Indeed, in the tree, their decision of exercising is based on different criteria.

There are two modeling methods for prepayments:

- The credit by credit method.

- The approach by credit pool when the homogeneous portfolio is large enough to reason in terms of percentage.

The credit by credit approach is used for the securities of corporate credit portfolios or project financing, generally of a larger size and in numbers that are too small for the application of the second method. This method has also been used for the RMBS when the pools were diverse and the models that gave the anticipated repayment probabilities needed to be calculated loan by loan. We typically note *h(t)* for the instant probability that the remaining capital *CRD(t)* will be repaid between *t* and *t+dt*, knowing that this was not the case beforehand. *m(t)* is the standard instalment amount without prepayment. *S(t)* is the survival function, that is the probability that a credit will not lead to a prepayment before *t*. We therefore have:

Formula 1: S(t) or the survival function

$$S(t) = e^{-\int_0^t h(u)\,du}$$

In *t*, apart from the risk of default and penalty, the bank receives:

$$\begin{cases} 0 \text{ if } t \geq T \text{ excluding default} \\ m(t) \text{ if reimbursements are normal with the probability } S(t).(1-h(t).dt) \\ m(t) + CRD(t) \text{ if prepayment with the probability } S(t).h(t).dt \end{cases}$$

This method is less adapted to a retail bank and relates more to financing and investment banks or to securitization.

The credit pooling method simply takes into account that a percentage *h(t)* of CRD(t) is repaid by anticipation on date t. It is adapted to major sized unified loan classes (over 1,000 loans). This is the method used in the models and output pricing of Freddy Mac and Fanny Mae.

The objective is to define the function h_t that gives the instantaneous percentage of prepayments at time t, that is to say the proportion of clients prepaying their loan according to all the information available on the rate curve since the beginning. It is clear that h_t will have a random combination linked to factors other than the rates that will be difficult to dissociate.

In any case, a rational and informed client will take the decision to exercise their repurchase option according to their forecast relative to market movements and historical details relating to the value difference between the actual price M_t (*id est* of the market), their financial product (the loan) and the price K_t that they need to pay when exercising their option. The function h_t therefore the most frequently uses as input either the difference $(M_t - K_t)$ or the ratio $\frac{M_t}{K_t}$.

In fact, the choice between these two expressions lies in the ability or not to take into account the scaling factor in the client's decision: clients do not behave in the same manner depending on the size of the remaining capital that is due. Those with larger amounts tend to behave more rationally. From there, the prepayment percentage during the time period dt becomes $S_t.h_t.dt$ and as the contracts draw closer to their maturity over time, h_s also tends to draw closer to zero. In the same manner, at 0, $h_0 = 0$.

The modeling of the function h_t has given rise to a number of studies where the main difficulty lies primarily in data collection. The best known market is the American mortgage market with four or five investment banks that maintain highly precise historical databases on their client behavior. With the crisis and the disappearance of two of these banks (Lehman and Bear), the data is less accessible (and less used, which is a pity as the reality remains the same). The American real estate loan market is also that which enabled the formalisation of the key definitions: SMM, CPR and PSA.

- SMM or 'Single Monthly Mortality' measures the prepayments percentage in the month relative to the theoretical nominal at the end of the month (that is to say before prepayments):

Formula 2: SMM

$$SMM = 1 - \frac{\text{end of month observed nominal}}{\text{end of month theoretical nominal}} = \frac{\text{prepayments of the month}}{\text{end of month theoretical nominal}}$$

- CPR, or Constant Prepayment Rate, measures the annual percentage of the nominal that will be repaid by anticipation if the prepayment rate adheres to the month's SMM. The CPR is therefore an annualised SMM:

Formula 3: CPR

$$CPR = \left[1 - (1 - SMM)^{12}\right]$$

- PSA (Public Standard Association) is a standardised series of CPR which defines a reference curve h_t for discussion among professionals (traders, bankers…). The PSA curve supposes the following:

- A linear growth of the CPRs from 0% to 6% over 30 months, i.e. +0.2% per month,
- Followed by stability over the next months.

Convention allows for the use of a single coefficient to roughly describe the prepayment speed of a pool. For example, 200 PSA means that the CPR doubles, passing from 0 to 12% in thirty months. The PSA curve is mainly used to calculate the prepayment rate of the American MBS and for discussion amongst traders. It is a model that is not generally adapted for RMBS modeling but as each institution usually keeps their model confidential, the method allows for a comparison of price from one single number.

Once the CPR(t) 'average' curve has been defined, the majority of models use a coefficient $k(t, r_{i,t})$ in the same way as for the PSA. $k(.)$ is a function of time and the rates curve that expresses the variations in this CPR curve according to a move in the interest rate.

Screenshot 3: Example of CPR settings in two temporal series: h(t) x coef(t, scenario i).

Description	St Di	Dura	Expiration Date	Coupon	Coupo Type	Fixing Type	Coupor Basis	Freque	Tax	Attri	CPR	CDR
Mortgages fixed rate		223		0.05	Fixed	In Ad..	A30360	Mon...	N...	In ...	coefRA*RA_Mortgages	cdR_mortgages
Mortgages fixed rate cst. pay		200		0.03937	Fixed	In Ad..	A30360	Mon...	N...	In ...	coefRA*RA_Mortgages	cdR_mortgages
Mortgages fixed rate amort. cst.		228		0.02997	Fixed	In Ad..	A30360	Mon...	N...	In ...	coefRA*RA_Mortgages	cdR_mortgages
Mortgages var. rate in fine		133		e3M	Floa..	In Ad..	ACT...	Mon...	N...	In ...	coefRA*RA_Mortgages	cdR_mortgages
Mortgages var. rate cst. pay		245		e3M	Floa..	In Ad..	ACT...	Mon...	N...	In ...	coefRA*RA_Mortgages	cdR_mortgages
Mortgages var. rate amort. cst.		330		e3M	Floa..	In Ad..	ACT...	Mon...	N...	In ...	coefRA*RA_Mortgages	cdR_mortgages
TOTAL (€)												

Theoretical optimum prepayment

In the loan contract, the client holds an American option C_t of the exercise price P_t that fluctuates over time and is similar to a bond option, more than a 'swaption', due to the fact the credit spread is included. In fact a loan relative to a bond is no more than another legal type for a receivable. The question of knowing when the client is interested in prepaying their loan is more complex than appears to be. A first reaction is to consider that, as it can be renegotiated as many times as wished, they should exercise their option as soon as they generate a minimum profit that covers the operational costs plus a certain margin (this one in a Cox-Ross model is the intrinsic value above the remaining value of the option). In truth it is difficult to refinance a 20 year loan more than two or three times, in the same way an institution that adds an anticipated repurchase clause to its bonds ('callable bonds') will not always exercise this clause as soon as it becomes profitable. It will wait until the profit reaches a size deemed sufficient enough before doing so. There is therefore an optimal repurchase date, depending on the client's anticipation regarding the movement of rates, their own spread and the market depth (that provides the necessary liquidity for repayments). There are two types of models:

- In the case that the formula is path dependent, calculations are extremely complex. The most advanced theories enable determining by estimation this date based on information available; they use stopping times mathematical theories on the Brownian movement and Snell enveloppes. The difficulty remains in the fact that, for example, in the model of Heath, Jarrow and Morton[8], a continuous model, which is relatively simple and offers the advantage of being close to the objective required for a direct correlation with the rate curve, there too the estimation is already quite complex. And it rarely takes into account the crossover effects of spread and rates (on the client spread and that of the bank). Practically, banks use Monte Carlo simulations to solve these problems most of the time but the calibration of the model is challenging and pricing can get far away from market prices.

- For formula independent of the path, tree models give good estimate specially if well calibrated to the market volatility curve. These models are most of the time sufficient and the only loss is the "media effect", which can be compensated for independently.

Even if formally the price estimate of the option requires a calculation for each credit, it is generally simpler to pool clients together by sub class and behavior.

Aggregated behaviors

Furthermore, the clients' behavior is not always rational, or, it depends on individual anticipations. Such anticipations are different for each client. For the crediting institution, clients appear as renegotiators in a fairly random sense around an unknown optimum value, which can lead to substantial gains. Some clients for example almost never renegotiate the conditions of their contracts. The previously mentioned function h_t has the objective of

---

[8] See *Notions in Financial Mathematics*

translating this phenomenon. Depending on the value of option C_t, it describes client behavior. The model here is very flexible even if it needs to remain within a certain number of constraints. In particular, $h_t(C_t)$ by definition is limited on $\mathcal{R}$ to $[0.1]$, rising (the higher the value of the option, more clients will decide to exercise it). Additionally, for negative values of the intrinsic value, we can assume h to be constant, or at least independent of the value of C_t and equal to k_t, a real element of $[0.1]$, eventually random itself and representing the structural prepayment rate.

Graph 3: prepayment rate h(C)

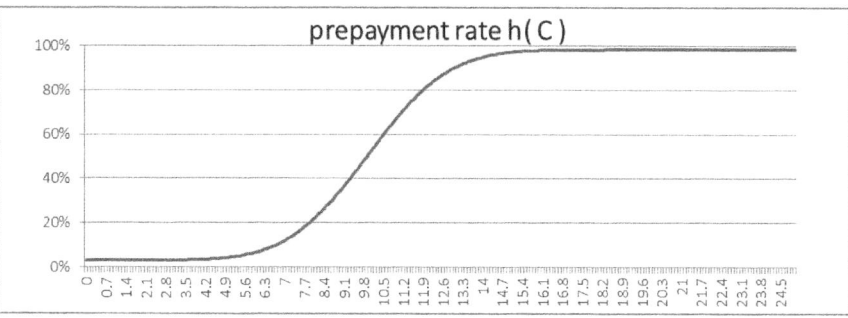

The key to the model lies in the fact that h_t depends on the rates via C_t. The choice between a model translating a direct or indirect dependence on interest rates will be dictated by the required information and the simplicity of the model.

h_t also depends on exogenous parameters that still allow for the calibration of the model: The percentage of prepayments said to be uncompressible k_t, the customer sensitivity to the valuation of their repurchase option, the efficiency of the network's persuasion concerning suggestions not to exercise the option… Also, as h_t depends on the clients' perception of the movements in rates, similarly, h_t depends on the past. Therefore, after a movement in interest rates, prepayments generally first increase and then come down.

Graph 4: instantaneous prepayment rate at C constant

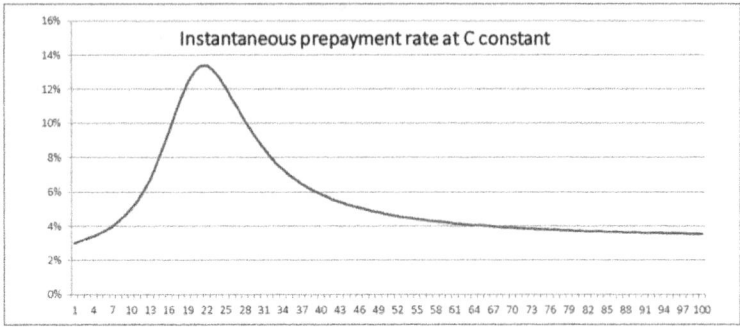

The number of clients chosing to exercise their option first increases then decreases towards the uncompressible rate. In fact, if after a certain amount of time, a client has not decided to exercise their option, it is certainly because they have not judged it advisable or anticipate a better period (in terms of being more micro-economic, the option's utility function does not justify the exercise). We could also model this by assuming that the prepayments, at constant C_t, depend on the history of C_t.

Pricing

To summarize, the American *pricing* option becomes the possibility of paying, at any time, the wealth Z_t as follows:

Formula 4: Z_t

$$Z_t = h_t.C_t.e^{-\int_0^t h_u.du}$$

The problem becomes a classic exercise (although complex) of *pricing* that modern pricing tools can resolve. One should note however that the price also depends on the underlying volatility (as customers display a period of latency before reacting, short volatility is therefore not appropriate).

As h_t increases with C_t, we obtain a continuum of emerging options: the more expensive the option, the higher the number of clients that repurchase their credit. In technical terms, the sensitivity (or modified duration) of a credit pool is variable: by convexity we mean the second derivation of price[9]. The credits are of a negative convexity:

- The more rates decrease, the more the clients prepay and the more the credit (or the MBS) duration decreases. It is clear that the discount factors of cash flows appreciate but as these cash flows decrease in duration, the price increases less than with the vanilla bond of a weak (and negative) convexity.

- Conversely, the more the rates increase, the less the clients prepay and the longer the credit pool duration becomes at the time when discount factors depreciate. Its price thus decreases faster than with a standard bond.

Table 2

IR	Bond in fine		Pool of linear amortizing loans (over 12 years)		
	price	modified duration	price	modified duration	CPR
1%	119.4%	4.544	115.30%	3.77	15.0%
2%	114.1%	4.489	111.94%	3.92	12.5%
3%	109.2%	4.435	108.4%	4.15	9.5%
4%	104.5%	4.382	104.4%	4.33	7.0%
5%	100.0%	4.329	100%	4.47	5.0%
6%	95.8%	4.278	95.56%	4.47	4.0%
7%	91.8%	4.227	91.31%	4.41	3.5%
8%	88.0%	4.177	87.34%	4.32	3.3%
9%	84.4%	4.128	83.64%	4.21	3.1%
10%	81.0%	4.080	80.17%	4.11	3.0%

The pricing of negative convexity is expressed via the spread that an RMBS pays in relation to a standard bond of the same sensitivity. It is in fact an interesting way of defining the cost of a prepayment option for the internal transfer rate (see related chapter).

---

[9] See *Notions in Financial Mathematics*, 1.1.7.1 page 34:

$$c = \frac{1}{P} \cdot \frac{\partial^2 P}{\partial r^2} \text{ et } P(r+dr) = P(r) \cdot \left[1 - s.dr + \frac{c}{2}.dr^2 + o(dr^2) \right]$$

Banks generally cover themselves against negative convexity by purchasing 'swaptions' in such a way that their NBI global variations remain within the limits they have fixed. The operations are therefore placed in macrohedging and the internal transfer rates are generally impacted as a pro-rata of the option premiums paid. There again, the superiority of a global modeling method of the balance sheet (therefore with the new production) is incontestable. In fact, if for example during a period of rising rates, there is a lack of profit with the stock, the new production is, itself, generally favored by the economic growth climate (the rates rise due to the anticipated inflation): retail banks are normally favored by a rise in long-term rates (as their retail resources are not very sensitive to interest rates in general). Investment banks need to be far more attentive to this phenomenon due to their variable refinancing rate (they generally lend for this at variable rates).

It should be noted that the covering strategies based on swaptions are incomplete if they do not completely integrate the correlation between the issuer's spread and that of the clients (or the retail client margin): during a recession, rates decrease, the clients repay faster, production slows and often, due to competition, client margins decrease[10] (at least at the beginning of the crisis). This effect reduces the NBI of the bank at the time when its own spread may rise due to the recession and therefore increases the cost of its market resources (as it was observed during the last crisis).

Having said that, the banks are structural option sellers, in the same way as they are structural liquidity transformers. Entirely covering this risk would make no sense, even more so as it should be analyzed as an element in the global balance sheet deviation. Finally, as the clients are not perfectly informed and trained to understand options theories, their exercises continue to exhibit unoptimized behavior that is to the benefit of the bank.

---

[10] The effect of decreasing margins due to the decrease in volumes can be observed mainly on the good quality retail files. It was balanced out during the crisis of 2008 by a general rise in spreads and the crunch of banking capacities. The phenomenon is therefore difficult to predict as it really depends on the global economic context.

Screenshot 4: *Modeling example taking into account the CPR and CDR*

	0	1	2	3	4	5	6	7	8	9
Interest Rate	3.94 %	3.94 %	3.94 %	3.94 %	3.94 %	3.94 %	3.94 %	3.94 %	3.94 %	
Current Nominal	400,000.00	395,597.33	389,844.14	384,164.19	378,556.63	373,019.98	367,551.91	363,362.72	359,211.95	35
Theorical Face	400,000.00	400,000.00	398,572.04	397,139.39	395,702.04	394,259.98	392,813.18	391,361.64	389,905.34	38
Default	0.00	124.00	124.94	124.10	123.25	123.03	124.34	122.52	121.12	
Standard Reimbursement	0.00	0.00	1,411.80	1,400.83	1,389.94	1,379.13	1,368.40	1,357.74	1,351.67	
Prepayments	0.00	4,278.67	4,216.45	4,155.02	4,094.37	4,034.48	3,975.34	2,708.93	2,677.99	
Recovery (with lag)	0.00	80.60	81.21	80.67	80.11	79.97	80.82	79.64	78.73	
Losses / Impairments	0.00	-43.40	-43.73	-43.44	-43.14	-43.06	-43.52	-42.88	-42.39	
CPR	12.84 %	12.84 %	12.84 %	12.84 %	12.84 %	12.84 %	8.88 %	8.88 %	8.88 %	
CDR	0.37 %	0.38 %	0.38 %	0.39 %	0.39 %	0.40 %	0.40 %	0.40 %	0.40 %	
LGD	35.00 %	35.00 %	35.00 %	35.00 %	35.00 %	35.00 %	35.00 %	35.00 %	35.00 %	
Cumulative Delinquencie...	0.00 %	0.03 %	0.06 %	0.09 %	0.12 %	0.15 %	0.19 %	0.22 %	0.25 %	
Cumulative Losses (on i...	0.00 %	0.01 %	0.02 %	0.03 %	0.04 %	0.05 %	0.07 %	0.08 %	0.09 %	
Cumulative CPR (on initi...	0.00 %	1.07 %	2.12 %	3.16 %	4.19 %	5.19 %	6.19 %	6.87 %	7.54 %	

Regarding new production

New production is obviously a factor in the increase of incertitude in modeling, as we know neither the exact volume nor the rates. It is also a delicate exercise in that the new credits amortize themselves, creating a cascade effect.

There are two methods for modeling new production:
1. The classic method consists in estimating the monthly production according to scenarios and then gradually integrating it into the balance sheet as it becomes reality. This method is the simplest. This has the advantage of being directly understandable and being

based on commercial forecast data. It should however then be modulated according to the scenario; in an aggravated crisis period the commercial objectives are not often attained. Moreover, the sales teams' estimations are generally used for reference purposes relative to variable bonuses or remunerations, they are therefore subject to caution. The person responsible for forecasting would do best to exercise caution and prudence.

2. The second solution is to work directly on the stock by simply supposing that a certain percentage of reimbursements is reinvested in new assets with new market conditions, assets which will amortize and in turn be reinvested. This method is more complex regarding the programing aspect due to the snowball effect of the revenue: a stock line created the first month that creates a line of new production that will itself start to amortize during the second month and is going to impact what is invested from the second month in a new line. However, once programed, it is simpler to implement because one simply needs to indicate the percentage to be reinvested. For loans of an initial duration of over a year, if the percentage is higher than 100%, the stock will grow immediately. If it is inferior to 100% then the stock will decrease[11]. The coefficient therefore enables the management of the stock. This method is interesting as it translates the commercial behavior of networks of which the objective is the growth of assets. It also enables comparison between the calculated projected production required for anticipated growth and the sales commercial objectives. It also has the advantage of not relying on the sales objectives; which is useful in long-term projections. In fact these commercial objectives are only defined for the coming year, occasionally for a two year estimate but rarely for three years. After this period, the stock roll methodology appears to be the most efficient.

In reality, banks therefore often use the first method for the following year and the second for the following years.

Screenshot 5: *Modeling example specifying a rule and ratio of a roll.*

---

[11] The coefficient has not been annualized. For example, for a stock of three months, a coefficient different to 100% such as 110% gives a non-annual quarterly growth rate, that is the stock one year after equals $110^4 = 146\%$

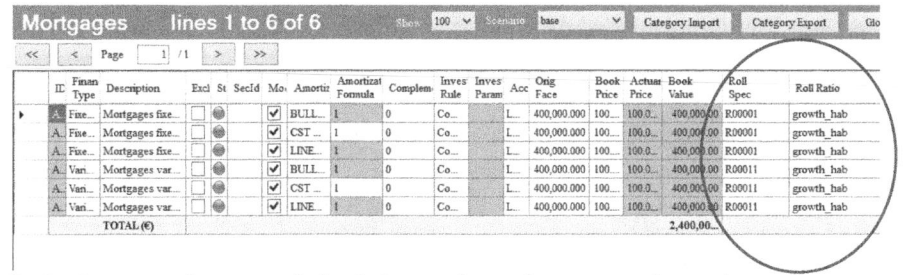

ID	Finan Type	Description	Excl	St	SecId	Mo	Amortiz	Amortizat Formula	Complem	Inves Rule	Inves Param	Acc	Orig Face	Book Price	Actual Price	Book Value	Roll Spec	Roll Ratio
A...	Fixe...	Mortgages fixe...	☐	●		✔	BULL...	1	0	Co...		L...	400,000.000	100...	100.0...	400,000.00	R00001	growth_hab
A...	Fixe...	Mortgages fixe...	☐	●		✔	CST...	1	0	Co...		L...	400,000.000	100...	100.0...	400,000.00	R00001	growth_hab
A...	Fixe...	Mortgages fixe...	☐	●		✔	LINE...	1	0	Co...		L...	400,000.000	100...	100.0...	400,000.00	R00001	growth_hab
A...	Vari...	Mortgages var...	☐	●		✔	BULL...	1	0	Co...		L...	400,000.000	100...	100.0...	400,000.00	R00011	growth_hab
A...	Vari...	Mortgages var...	☐	●		✔	CST...	1	0	Co...		L...	400,000.000	100...	100.0...	400,000.00	R00011	growth_hab
A...	Vari...	Mortgages var...	☐	●		✔	LINE...	1	0	Co...		L...	400,000.000	100...	100.0...	400,000.00	R00011	growth_hab
		TOTAL (€)														2,400,00...		

In both cases, the part of the balance sheet that comes from the new production should be clearly separated from the stock for several reasons:

- It is important to foresee stock renewal over time. Its growth is more random, requires more hypothesis and the direction can particularly influence the development of its size.

- In this manner it is important to understand the part of the NBI coming from this new activity. The two quantities, balance sheet and NBI, give an indication of the balance sheet renewal rythm; after how much time does the remaining stock become less than 10% of the NBI? We can observe a cycle close to that of the economic cycle of private banks; after 5 years, new production becomes prominant in credit and after 7 years it becomes prominant in NBI.

- Clearly separating the stock also enables the visualisation of the 'in stock' situation which management is more passive over the coming years.

Screenshot 6: *Example of a roll result: The balance sheet line and interest income of the Roll are well separated. The new production is shown in the window through successive layers that are themselves amortized and rolled again.*

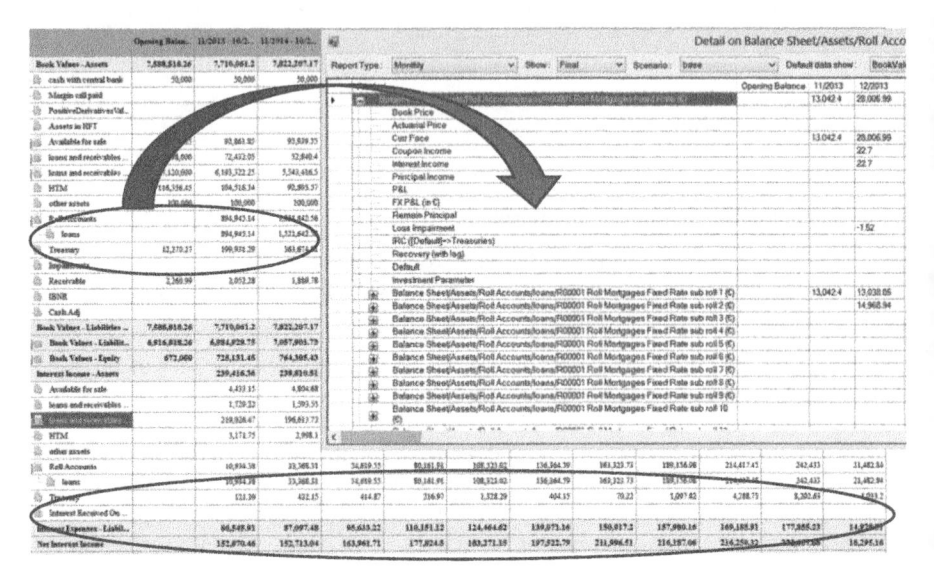

The variables that contribute to model the new production are normally the volumes and the rates. The duration characteristics are often heavy trends, fairly well managed by banks since the crisis made them aware of the consequences of lending long[12]. To that can be added the fact that the regulators are starting to put a brake on the banks lending real estate loans longer term as this is one of the major factors in the formation of real estate bubbles in low housing availability zones.

Credit rates depend on three factors:

- Market rates
- Cost of bank refinancing. This factor is the object of constant internal debates (see the chapter on internal rates of cession). It is generally the cash rate (and not the CDS as this can show

---

[12] Before the crisis, the credit durations had strongly risen, a movement that favoured the creation of speculative bubbles on unbalanced real estate markets at the advantage of the sellers due to the shortage of offers. On real estate market, this phenomena is even more important since the bank offer has the clear role of a moderator.

considerable variations[13]), taking into account the options cost on a statistical basis.

- Commercial margin. This includes competitive pressure.

Graph 5: In this (real) example, the new production is prominent after 7 years.

example of balance-sheet evolution

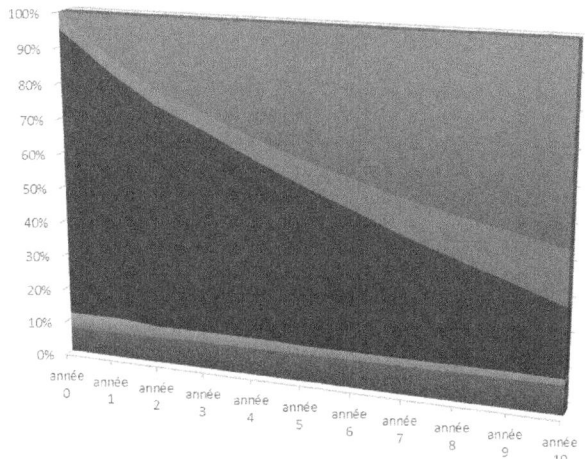

Assets AFS ■ Loans and receivables to financial inst. ■ Loans and receivables to customers ■ treasury ■ New production

Passage to a continuous model

The credits with constant monthly repayments are the essential part of a bank balance sheet at a fixed rate for, as an example, the French banks. This is why it is interesting to undertake a short methodological digression in order to understand the impact of prepayments via continuous time. The uninterrupted model also enables a simple analysis[14] of the stock effects on a balance sheet and calculations relative to sensitivity.

---

[13] See *Notions in Financial Mathematics*, chapter 4.2.2. Link between z-spread and CDS spread.
[14] For a bank that produces constant monthly credits every day for an initial duration of 15 years for example, the continuous modeling will not be bad if the realisation rates remain constant.

If we use the example of a credit pool with constant prepayments, for an initial duration T, an interest rate of r and the initial nominal CRD(0) = 1. We have a trivial CRD(T) = 0.

Exclusive of anticipated repayments, we therefore have the immediate monthly payments at t $m.dt$ corresponding to:

- the repayment of the principal: $-dCRD(t)$
- and the interest payments $r.CRD(t).dt$

Formula 5

$$m.dt = -dCRD(t) + r.CRD(t).dt$$

The solution of this differential equation is in the following form:

Formula 6

$$CRD(t) = \left(1 - \frac{m}{r}\right).e^{r.t} + \frac{m}{r}$$ in order to satisfy CRD(0)=1

The constraint at expiry of CRD(T)=0 implies

$$m = \frac{r}{1 - e^{-r.T}}$$

And
$$CRD(t) = \frac{1 - e^{-r.(T-t)}}{1 - e^{-r.T}}$$

$$dCRD(t) = \frac{-r.e^{-r.(T-t)}}{1 - e^{-r.T}}.dt$$

$$\frac{dCRD(t)}{CRD(t)} = \frac{-r.e^{-r.(T-t)}}{1 - e^{-r.(T-t)}}.dt$$

The credit price at time t for an instantaneous rate of x is worth:

Formula 7

$$P(t,x) = m.\int_t^T e^{-x.u}.du = m.\frac{e^{-x.t} - e^{-x.T}}{x} = \frac{r}{x} . \frac{e^{-x.t} - e^{-x.T}}{1 - e^{-r.T}}$$

And the modified duration:

Formula 8 & 9: modified duration

More specifically:
$$-\frac{\partial \ln P(t,x)}{\partial x} = \frac{1}{x} - \frac{T.e^{-x.T} - t.e^{-x.t}}{e^{-x.t} - e^{-x.T}}$$

$$-\frac{\partial \ln P(t=0, x=r)}{\partial x} = \frac{1}{r} - \frac{T}{e^{r.T} - 1}$$

In particular:

Table 3: *Rate sensitivity after integration of the prepayment rate for a constant monthly credit.*

Duration T / rate r	3%	5%	10%
5	2.4	2.4	2.3
10	4.8	4.6	4.2
15	6.9	6.6	5.7
20	9.0	8.4	6.9
25	11.0	10.0	7.8

The expressions have the great advantage of enabling very simple calculations. Therefore the stock at *t* of a bank producing 1 at each moment *u* is constant:

Formula 9: stock

$$stock(t) = \int_{t-T}^{t} CRD(t, \text{expiring date } u+T).du = \int_{t-T}^{t} \frac{1-e^{-r.(T+u-t)}}{1-e^{-r.T}}.du$$

$$stock(t) = \int_{0}^{T} \frac{1-e^{-r.v}}{1-e^{-r.T}}.dv \text{ with } v = T+u-t$$

$$stock = \frac{T}{1-e^{-r.T}} - \frac{1}{r}$$

The effects on stock are however always gradually distributed.

Therefore, the expressed derivative always gives the stock sensitivity at a variation of the rate but this will not impact entirely the stock before its complete renewal, that is after a duration of T.

Let us now suppose an anticipated prepayment rate $h(t).CRD(t).dt$ at time t, the equation on the capital amortization will be modified due to this supplementary parameter which will impact the nominal on the instantaneous payments. The capital variation remaining of $CRD(t)$ comes from normal reimbursements on the remaining nominal and prepayments:

Formula 10

$$-dCRD(t) = \frac{r.e^{-r(T-t)}}{1-r^{-r(T-t)}}.CRD(t).dt + h(t).CRD(t).dt$$

Where
$$\ln CRD(t) = -r.\int_0^t \frac{e^{r.u}}{e^{r.T} - e^{r.u}}.du - \int_0^t h(u).du$$

$$\ln CRD(t) = \left[\ln\left(e^{r.T} - e^{r.u}\right)\right]_0^t - \int_0^t h(u).du$$

$$CRD(t) = \frac{1-e^{-r(T-t)}}{1-e^{-r.T}}.e^{-\int_0^t h(u).du}$$

The formula replicates the expression excluding anticipated prepayments multiplied by the survival function.

Graph 6: *Profile of an amortization on a 20 year constant monthly credit according to a prepayment rate.*

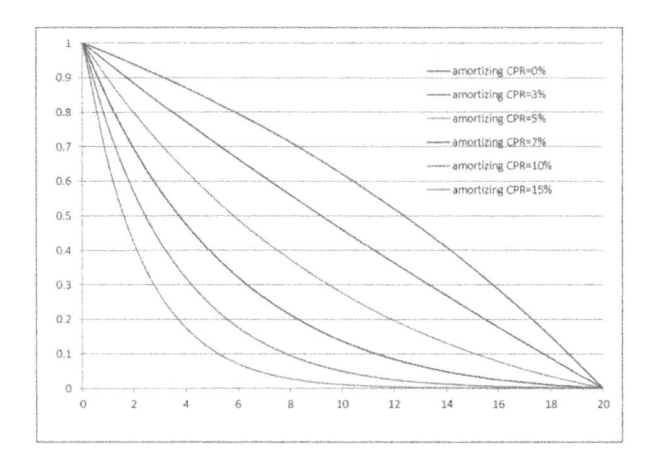

Assets and liabilities in currencies

The provision of credit in foreign currencies, like all other lines in foreign currency, poses the problem of modeling the exchange rate and its impact. Each scenario relating to the relevant currency should supply an exchange rate trajectory and rate curve (from 5 to 10 variables to be modeled). The modeling should furthermore replicate the FX accounting rules for the processing of underlying P&L.

It does only however refer to a supplementary asset to model. The great difficulty is more in the analysis and particularly the increase in risk taken by the bank as in general it has more difficulties refinancing with foreign currency, is not always a member of the foreign system of the central bank and finally has less experience with the credit risk of clients, in particular on the impact of exchange rates on their ability to repay. This latter point is obviously fundamental and highly correlated in most cases. In fact, the falling of a currency is often associated with the economic breakdown of a state or country. These catastrophic scenarios should therefore be examined separately in the form of stress-tests by requiring them to foresee the different measures taken by the authorities; freezing assets, forced mergers...

Participations raise the problem of hedging the capital of the foreign subsidiary. The subject is particularly complex for investments in emerging countries with strong growth and inflation. Inflation erodes the nominal in terms of the purchasing power of the original currency so pushing it to a lower exchange rate (the purchasing power parity gives a trend around the differential of inflation reduced by the differential of GDP growth). On the contrary, economic growth tends to break the trend of a fall in exchange rate. Finally, in the absence of a credit mishap, the growth of incomes (due to inflation and economic growth, and often an increase in the banking sector) is supposed to more than compensate for loss in the initial exchange. In reality, the first risk in this kind of investment is macroeconomic (and geostrategic). Certain emerging economies are strongly tied to a single economic factor, the most common being the price of oil. The implementation of a hedge will therefore have two objectives:

- hedging the investment against a major crisis: this represents buying protection that is strongly out of the money.
- Covering the erosion of capital during the investment return period: the protection will have the objective of stabilizing the

investment return in Euros for the duration of the initial business plan (generally 3 to 5 years).

The risk of exchange rate is one of the most delicate and the most random. Defining an intelligent hedging strategy requires a meticulous modeling and advanced macro-economic study. Still remains a high uncertainty with the effects of anticipation, the market, arbitrage of rates that often counteract the macro-economic fundamentals and of course interventions from the central banks. Inflation, interest rates, and exchange rates are correlated over the long term but over the short term, in other words a few years, we often observe a considerable divergence. Therefore in the absence of a strong conviction on the future movements it is wise to systematically cover the FX risk over a significant horizon.

Deposits of undefined maturity

Deposits of undefined maturity are the subject of a long debate on their accountability, stability and modeling. The debate is fuelled by the methodology called 'static gap', implicitly validated by the regulator, which imposes an amortization rule on the deposit.

The subject mainly concerns cash deposits but also savings accounts and all products without regular instalments of a commercial 'retail' bank. From a statistical viewpoint, it refers to all M1 monetary aggregates (composed of 80% cash deposits and 20% bank funds) and M2 (M1 plus the projected deposits of less than 3 months and bonds of less than 2 years). Historically, central banks have always attentively followed their monetary aggregates even if the link between credit and money supply is complex and they profess to pay little regard to it relative to inflation guidance[15]. From an economic perspective, the classic school of thought link inflation to the quantity of money in circulation (through the proceeds of the monetary amount by its circulation speed). This link has been the subject of numerous studies that give a long-term relation that is difficult to analyze as there are

---

[15] This paragraph does not discuss the connection between inflation and monetary mass, the reader is referred for this to other leading macro-economic literature on the subject. Where the causes of inflation are as in the classic monetary model, the rise in the monetary mass or where other factors enter into account (services inflation, exterior shocks, fiscal and budgetary policies, progress...), the fact is that inflation is translated into a growth in M1.

many factors to take into consideration. Some of the trends however are generally held to be as follows:

- The most important is that M1 follows closely the growth of an economy and even if the variations are of a larger size than the GDP variations, it is still a very stable aggregate; there are no variations at the fall that are strong enough to endanger the financial system in a normal period. In the 2008 crisis this aggregate in fact remained within the realms of historical volatility. From a regulator's point of view or that of a group with a significant market share (more than 5%), the collective deposits are probably the most stable resource of a commercial bank's activities if it is real retail clients (that have deposited their incomes in the bank). Also, due to its indexation regarding growth and its low or zero cost (exclusive of network cost), it is probably the central resource of the banking sector.

Graph 7: M1 and inflation in France

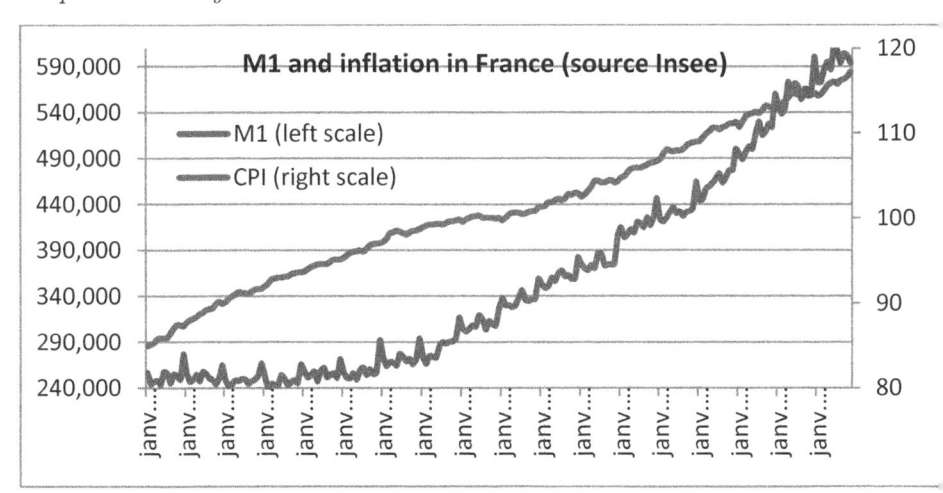

M1 generally grows faster than inflation. This probably translates into the acceleration phenomenon of currency circulation in modern economies and a better use of it. This rule may have its limits and certainly dates back to the exceptional growth period experienced by the Western economies since the Second World War. It is not perfect with an M1/GDP ratio that has fluctuated over the last twenty years and a period of stability of M1 in the western European economies at the beginning of the 90s due to short-term high interest rates. Statistical regressions between M1 and the inflation rate show a fair correlation over the period starting after the petrol crisis up to the start of the euro.

M1 has the tendency to grow less rapidly during recessions due to a slowing of credit.

M1 is sensitive to interest rates, the economic agents conducting arbitrage during the period of high interest rates towards investments with a higher return such as observed after the German reunification at the beginning of the 90's. On the contrary, during a period of low interest rates, they leave their savings in their current account. This phenomenon has an inverse effect to that previous one as periods of growth and inflation are themselves correlated. As transfers are generally carried out between M1 and M2, the effect is weak overall for a bank. In the beginning of the 90's, it regarded more the treasury's bond funds (M3 being outside the banks' balance sheet).

M1 shows a cyclical nature linked to the household lifestyle: Holidays, back to school, end of year festivities, tax period… A cycle that is easy to follow and predictable.

Graph 8: M1 Eurozone

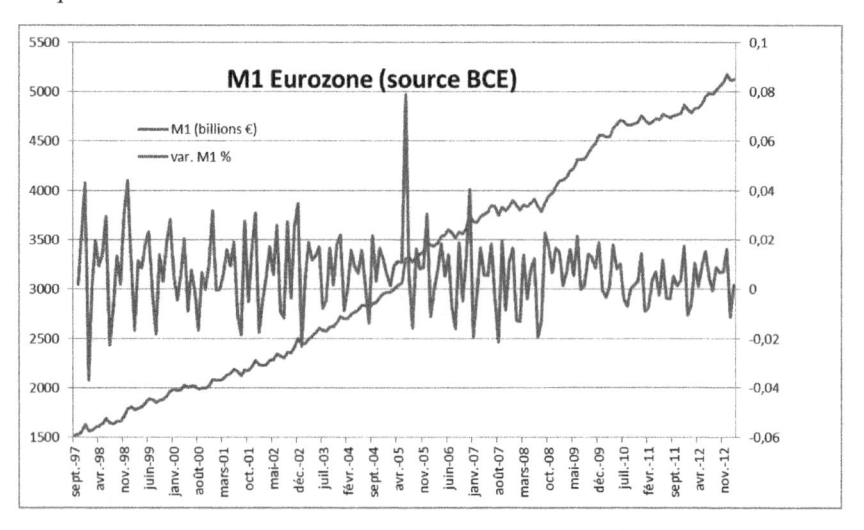

The most important point of these observations is simply that a fixed rule such as the depreciation of deposits cannot have an econometric foundation based on the M1 statistics series. It refers to a conventional decision taken in concurrence with other criteria[16].

On the scale of an institution, it is interesting to note that we can observe the same impossibility of basing an amortization rule for cash deposits on past statistical behavior. The chart below displays a daily series over a long period for a classic banking establishment. The analysis of the cash deposits movements shows a number of cycles:

- Cyclicity for a week, shopping mainly occurring Saturday and Wednesday.
- Monthly cyclicity between the beginning and the end of the month.
- Annual cyclicity already mentioned (taxes, holidays, back to school, festivities...)

It equally represents a great stability that is implicitly recognized by the regulator in the LCR ratio it places the stable part of individuals' deposits under the deposits guarantee by a reduction hypothesis of 5% for a major crisis scenario.

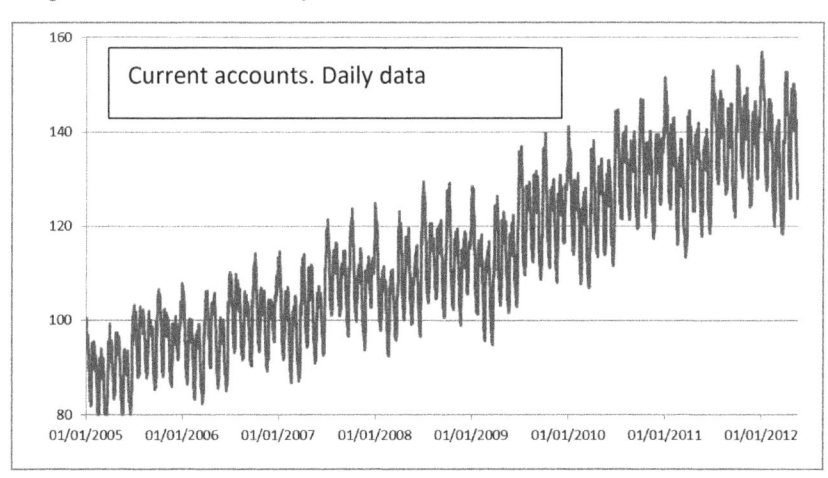

Graph 9: current accounts daily data

---

[16] The most logical is the purely mathematical argument of stock/collect homogeneity that is used to recommend exponential amortizing.

The micro-economic analysis on working professionals gives a more volatile series with a more rational treasury management (investment at the end of the month of the surplus, management of the 31st December) but with similar and symmetrical characteristics (the tradespeople being beneficiaries of the product sales).

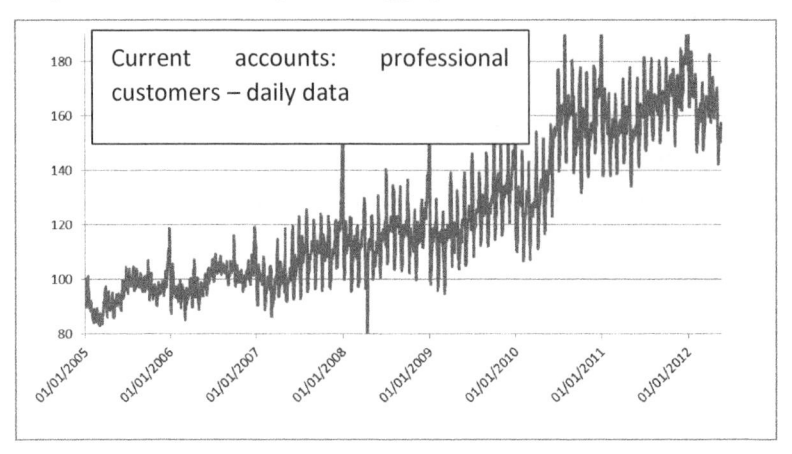

Graph 10: current accounts for working professionals

[Chart: Current accounts: professional customers – daily data, showing values from approximately 80 to 180 over dates from 01/01/2005 to 01/01/2012]

In the standard operating configuration of an institution's activity, the cash deposits are normally modelled as a random stock that grows in line with a general trend and also undergoes behavioral phenomena around this trend.

In a crisis configuration, the withdrawal behavior relating to deposits is another problem:

- Bear Stearns found itself in a payment default position within twenty minutes following the withdrawal of two large clients whose deposits totalled several billions. Their decision was motivated by the fact that at market values, Bear had lost its own capital due to the underlying losses in its portfolio for Freddy Mac and Fanny Mae[17]. This type of rational behavior from institutions and large businesses explains the regulator's choice in supposing that for the LCR institutional deposits leave entirely in times of crisis and those of corporations leave heavily.

---

[17] Concerning the fall of Bear, see 'House of Cards'

- Private banks experience a similar problem with a rapid withdrawal risk on their deposits in case of reputational problems and regulatory or fiscal changes. In this case, modeling withdrawal should take more into account client diversification per country and their reasons for investment in a private bank: secure residents savings in a politically fragile country or one subject to severe violence (ransom payments, inheritance protection, possible preparation for fleeing), fiscal optimization (or fraud), anxiety relative to service discretion and quality, protection of savings judged to be at risk (risk of confiscation due to taxes, frozen assets...). We can observe the same problem relating to the deposits concentration concerning some particular type of clientele as in France with the CDC where the notary deposits have strongly fallen (-25%) during the crisis.

Finally, institutions are always at the mercy of regulatory changes that can cause a run on savings product deposits. The latter scenario should however be balanced by the fact that the legislative bodies gain nothing long-term by destabilising their financial sector and the savings of their fellow citizens.

In both cases, current activity or crisis scenario, the static modeling that consists in amortizing deposits doesn't have any fundamental econometric base on the observed past behavior or behavior model of deposit withdrawals. It can even not really be justified by imagining a very long-term run-off scenario for an institution, as such a scenario is unrealistic. Either the institution would close and it would transfer its deposits or require its clients to do the same, or it would maintain its activity and accept additional deposits, which makes an existing stock model pointless due to repayments and new flow. Indeed only a global modeling of the stock appears adapted.

As it turns out, static modeling is derived from two other motivations:
- The first pertains to liquidity. A loan production business strategy needs to be defined. The strategy should be stable, sustainable and balanced while keeping true to the characteristics of current and savings accounts. It must be designed for the long-term sustainability of the bank, so that the institution may survive in the event of a crisis or of unexpected regulatory changes.
- The second relates to the "fragmented bank" methodology (refer to the NBI analysis chapter): ALM requires benchmarks to be defined with regards to the investment deposits of unspecified

maturity. This ensures that business income is as stable as possible while in parallel it provides an assessment opportunity of its contribution to banking income against these benchmarks (refer to the chapter on internal rates).

This has an effect on both the management of interest rate risk and bank liquidity risk. It leads back to the discussion on the preferred use of static or dynamic gaps, which we will address at a later stage. In real life we can say that modeling should include two phases:

- Modeling economic reality results in an outstanding stock with no maturity that fluctuates according to the scenario.

- Regulations and reinvestment constraints for the assets are conducive to defining target benchmarks strategies for reinvestment.

Screenshot 7: Modeling current accounts with an undefined maturity date or "no maturity" with a time series to provide a model of their evolution per scenario "growth_dav" and with a vector that defines their target reinvestment convention "amort_current"

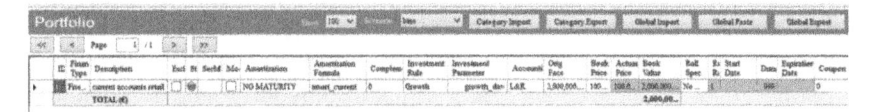

Other balance sheet items

Securities and off-balance sheet items

Securities are the simplest assets to deal with since there is abundant literature on their pricing. To incorporate them line by line is generally easier and more precise. Yet an exception to this is large-sized portfolios. In the case of such sizes, developing a market benchmark is relevant, even if some extra alpha and beta is required. This approach is valid for off-balance sheet items.

The ALM model is not meant to replace the pricing system on risk computing chains. Given the amount of unknowns that ALM must manage, a lower degree of accuracy is not only tolerated but is expected. It must be in a position to provide a sound estimate of the impact of the movement of funds: distortions in the yield curve, variations in spread and volatility or potentially even in correlation.

Each institution will select a level of accuracy tailored to the requirements of its primary activity:

- A reasonable level of accuracy can be provided for standard bonds. It is obtained from a pricer that updates future cash flow on the zero-coupon curve, potentially with a changing spread over time (in addition to its variability per scenario). Variation in bond spreads can be modeled per scenario with the use of conventional methods:

Formula 11

$$S_{bond}(t) = \alpha_{bond} + \beta_{bond,bench} \cdot S_{bench}(t)$$

The price of the bond becomes, by referring to CF_i as the perceived cash flow and s_i as the spread of the risked[18] zero-coupon bond at time t:

Formula 12

$$V_t = \sum_{i=1}^{N} \frac{CF_i}{(1+r_{t,t_i}+s_i)^{(t_i-t)}}$$

- The same beta method may be adapted to share stocks.

Formula 13

$$ER_i = r + \frac{\text{cov}(R_i, R_m)}{VR_m} \cdot (ER_m - r) \text{ with } \beta_i = \frac{\text{cov}(R_i, R_m)}{VR_m}$$

Screenshot 8 : Simple model of an HFT share certificate, setting its value as the function of a stock benchmark: it is important not to multiply settings

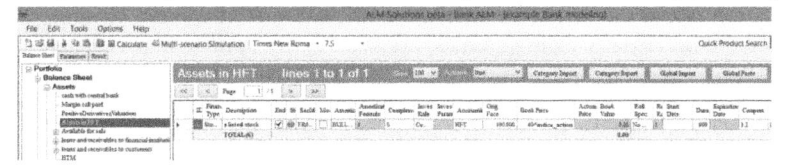

- Just like their benchmark, funds are modeled. With our global approach, they are integrated to the overall interest rate and liquidity risk. Why do we use this approach? Simply because they are there. Implying that integrating them is redundant given that it incorporates the decisions of a fund manager to whom this task was delegated does not necessarily mean that they should be

---

18 Moulin (2012), p.117-118

excluded from overall measurements. Indeed the fund manager's added value is his or her capacity to succeed above and beyond his or her benchmark due to tactical choices. And this we cannot model. Yet the choice of benchmark-based investment strategy falls under the ALM umbrella. It is then only its management that is delegated. The fund is part of the bank's global interest rate risk to the same extent as the lines that treasury actively manages. Thus the ALM department needs to integrate the funds to the exposure calculations. ALM department's role is then to ensure for each term that the position chosen based on this benchmark remains a valid one. If it does not hold anymore, ALM department can reduce the exposure or adjust other asset classes in the global allocation. As such the approach is not contradictory.

- With regards to complex bonds and off-balance sheet products, what matters is to find the right balance between accuracy and calculation complexity. As a general rule, as soon as an analytical formula such as a B&S or an HJM formula can be used, then it must be used. The smile/skew effects can be roughly approximated. Assets that are path-dependent (extension options, callable, corridors or activating barriers...) are more sensitive. One approach is to set their value separately and to then add those values back into the scenario. Another approach is to use these initial simulations to find an analytical formula that would work for the set of scenarios. In any case, it is always best to apply the exact model to those assets that have non-linear cash-flows. Thus options, caps or floors, must be modelled with real formulas for coupons - such as $max(strike, E3M)$ - and B&S type classic pricing, even if the parameters are rough estimations. This is preferable to applying linear formulas that are derived from deltas (or potentially from gammas) and that apply to only slight changes[19].

- Exotic formulas of the type snowball, reverse floater, corridor and expendable nominal ... must be the focus of greater attention. Ethics dictates that these formulas do not belong to a client's balance sheet, no matter who the client is. These formulas tend to primarily give the structuring bank the capacity to hide undue margins, and provide an opportunity to up-front option premiums to the unscrupulous client. Unless they are to be micro-swapped,

---

[19] Regulatory authorities are cautious with regards to the way options are handled with the ALM model. Refer to Basel Committee on Banking Supervision (2004), p.29: "...the risk of options may not be adequately captured".

these formulas do not belong to a bank's balance sheet. If it is not the case, an adapted pricer must be developed to price hidden options adequately.

Screenshot 9 : Complex coupon model example

Dura	Expiration Date	Coupon
82	11/07/2...	E3M+1.4%
78	02/03/2...	E3M+1.485%
91	06/04/2...	Max(0.0175,Min(1.77*CMS2Y,0.06))
92	15/05/2...	Max(0.0175,Min(1.75*CMS2Y,0.0565))
92	10/05/2...	Max(2.7%,Min(9.9%,9.9%-Max(5%+10*Min(CMS10Y-CMS2Y,12%)-CMS10Y,0)))
93	30/06/2...	Max(3%,Min(9.91%,9.91%-20*abs(CMS10Y_decal1Y-CMS2Y_decal1Y-(CMS10Y-CMS2Y))))

Complex coupon model example: all formulas can be adequately modeled in CF even if at times they require the use of dynamic variables (recurrences, conditionals).

Fixed assets, intangible assets, tax assets ...

Except for goodwills, these lines are usually independent of economic scenarios. The sole purpose of including them in the balance sheet is to reconcile with the books and records and to guarantee that each line has been analysed and that its evolution has been modeled.

IFRS regulations are particularly dangerous for institutions when it comes to goodwill. When faced with the early stages of an economic downturn, institutions tend to exhibit a tendency for inertia. They unfortunately rarely react and adjust both their business plan and the corresponding valuations to the new set of parameters. This is even more the case for goodwill relating to acquisitions and operations made on the basis of a high economic cycle, for which the corresponding valuations have now become excessive. Auditors, whose role is not to anticipate fund trends, often act in successive stages. They start by asking questions, they then express reservations, and finally, they make institutions review their estimates. Often, of course, this occurs when the crisis has set in and the institution is struggling. These aspects must be integrated to the development of crisis scenarios. Even if this has no impact on solvency ratios, to prepare an action plan on "write downs" helps avoiding forward leakage where, the institution, unwilling or uncapable of cutting its losses, desperately maintains its position. Generally, it only gets worse until the institution throws in the towel at a much higher cost.

Static or dynamic gaps

ALM is often divided according to proponents of one or the other type of gap analysis:

- Proponents of **dynamic** gap analysis – who simulate balance sheet and income statement by taking into account new loan production and assuming steady business activity for the bank for years to come. Proponents of this approach consider it to be the closest to real life. They further adopt the view that it is the only approach to provide an answer to management's core question of whether "interest rates shift by X% and projections of the business plan in terms of production and deposit collection are met, by how much will incomes be affected?". Proponents of static gap analysis consider this method to be built on too many assumptions. A bank's balance sheet is commonly and almost always entirely renewed after five to seven years for its moving part. The efficiency of the dynamic methology is further deplored by its opponents for the complexity of its implementation. Indeed, the renewal of each credit line results in the production of new loans that have each their own amortization schedule.

- Proponents of **static** gap analysis - assume that since future loan production is unknown, it doesn't have to be taken into account. They consider that it can be hedged at a later stage. Proponents of this approach operate in a "compartmentalized bank" approach and define a convention of amortization for deposits without maturity (mainly current accounts). Proponents of dynamic gap analysis criticize static gap analysis for being far removed from reality as well as for transferring part of the loan production interest rate risk onto commercial business lines. It is also disapproved for banning accurate liquidity analysis, for its excessive arbitrary use of amortization conventions and for inaccurate interest rate risk analysis methodology. Proponents of static gap analysis approve especially two of its characteristics: there is no need to model NBI, which has been considered in the past a near-impossible task given how cumbersome back-office channels are. And it has been approved by regulatory authorities.

Both methods have long been presented as competing when in fact they are complementary. Both study the same portfolio of assets, one through a snapshot at a given point in time and the other through its recurrent activities. Static gap analysis was historically the first to be developed since, at the time, access to reliable data to model the overall bank was challenging. The regulator was pragmatic, accepting the method without really getting into scientific debate. It remains watchful with regards to conventions and especially their untimely modification which generally disguises a reversal of hedging positions rather than a structural change in the stability of current accounts.

In actual fact, the two methods differ in their purpose and their respective limits have to be clearly understood by finance directors and senior management. Beyond the incomplete methodological arguments that can at times be heard, the major issue in this debate is the confusion in the function of these two methods and the danger inherent in placing one against the other (essentially the static gap analysis method) into some sort of dogma that cannot be analyzed or explained, let alone challenged[20]. There is actually no reason for controversy here since measuring interest rate risk and defining a strategy to protect against these risks are two different matters. The best way to illustrate this perspective is to analyze each method separately.

Reconciling dynamic and static gap analysis

The two methods can be reconciled in a simple manner. To reconcile them, one needs to process new business separately. This way, the effects of reinvestments, of new business growth, and of the potential new reinvestment assumptions can be defined and monitored separately. The lack of activation of new business gives rise to "gross" static gaps, that is to say static gaps before any convention on the disposal of assets or of liabilities of indefinite duration. Static gaps allow for an initial insight into liquidity

---

[20] A 1930 text by Fisher expresses a similar attitude when presenting his MLE method and effectively challenging the Bayesian method, qoted by Armatte (1988, p.80) and translated here: "I know of one case only in mathematics of a doctrine that was accepted and developed by the most respected men of the times, and that may still be recognized as valid by their contemporaries, but which seemed at the same time to a number of esteemed writers to be fundamentally faulty and devoid of all foundations".

risk whereas dynamic gaps provide an opportunity for reinvestment risk (yield / interest rate, spread…) anticipation.

We get standard static gap analysis by fixing runoff conventions for indefinite term assets or liabilities. This analysis can then be completed with dynamic analysis by using the reinvestment rules for new business from funds of indefinite term.

Static gaps do differentiate between yield gaps and liquidity gaps so it is possible to reconcile the two methods. This requires discipline in modeling it. This can become quite a complex if one takes into account the whole evolution of the balance sheet:

- liabilities that run off according to conventions - for instance current accounts - must roll over onto themselves (that is to say that fall-off is reinvested into a new production of the same product) so that stock progress can be traced when outstanding amortization of new business is taken into account.
- In interest rate gaps, floating assets and liabilities are removed after the renewal of the coupon. Also, a quarterly floating rate credit duration of 24 months should be modeled just as a 3 months fixed credit rate that is replaced by a new 21 months loan at floating rate, a model that is heavy in terms of implementation.
- In liquidity gap analysis, one must not roll over floating rates in a manner that is different to rolling over fixed interest rates.

We get static gaps by freezing new business. By integrating new business to the model, the hold on new business is lifted and we get dynamic gap analysis. Liquidity and yield effects on these rollovers are clearly different to stock run-off. The concept may seem somewhat abstract. There has been much debate on the topic, much of which had little scientific basis. A simple scenario follows for the sake of clarity.

A simple scenario

Let us take the case of a bank that holds current accounts and a stock of linear amortizing loans over 5 years, half of which are at floating rate (Euribor 1 year) and the other at fixed rates. It maintains outstanding loans through the production of new loans. Its balance sheet will look as follows by differentiating the new loan production stock:

Table 4: The bank's balance sheet over five years in dynamic gap analysis (including the production of new loans)

			initial	yr 1	yr 2	yr 3	yr 4	yr 5
assets			200	200	200	200	200	200
fixed rate loans			100	100	100	100	100	100
		stock	100	80	60	40	20	0
	new production		0	20	40	60	80	100
Floating rate loans			100	100	100	100	100	100
		stock	100	80	60	40	20	0
	new production		0	20	40	60	80	100
liabilities	current accounts		200	200	200	200	200	200

For the institution income statement calculation to be exact, each year's new business must be amortized. By induction, we obtain the required production of new loans necessary for stock stability:

Table 5: New business per vintage

yr 1 production	20.0	16.0	12.0	8.0	4.0
yr 2 production		24.0	19.2	14.4	9.6
yr 3 production			28.8	23.0	17.3
yr 4 production				34.6	27.6
yr 5 production					41.5
Total new production	20.0	40.0	60.0	80.0	100.0

Increase in new loan production business for stock sustainability is required due to the self-amortizing nature of the previous years' loan production levels. The bank would be again in a steady-state at new annual production of 33.33 following a few years.

Calculating NBI requires the same breakdown per fixed-rate loan vintage whereas floating rate loans do not require this attention to detail given that annual interest rate applies overall to their case. Let us then assume the following variation in fixed rates (usually long) and short term rates and deduce its NBI:

Table 6: Income statement

	initial	yr 1	yr 2	yr 3	yr 4	yr 5
floating rate	4%	3%	5%	2%	1%	1%
fixed rate	6%	4%	4%	3%	3%	3%
fixed rate loans NBI	**6.0**	**5.6**	**5.2**	**4.5**	**3.8**	**3.1**
stock	6	4.8	3.6	2.4	1.2	0
new production		0.8	1.6	2.1	2.6	3.1
floating rate loans NBI	**4.0**	**3.0**	**5.0**	**2.0**	**1.0**	**1.0**
stock	4	2.4	3	0.8	0.2	0
new production	0	0.6	2	1.2	0.8	1
NBI TOTAL	**10.0**	**8.6**	**10.2**	**6.5**	**4.8**	**4.1**

The income statement shows that the asset is fully renewed after a few years: it is also possible to break down the NBI share coming from new loan production from the one coming from stock.

The NBI on fixed-rate loans arises from the breakdown per vintage:

Table 7: NBI of new business per vintage

	rate	yr 1	yr 2	yr 3	yr 4	yr 5
year 1 production	4%	0.8	0.6	0.5	0.3	0.2
year 2 production	4%		1.0	0.8	0.6	0.4
year 3 production	3%			0.9	0.7	0.5
year 4 production	3%				1.0	0.8
year 5 production	3%					1.2
New production total NBI	**4.0**	**3.0**	**5.0**	**2.0**	**1.0**	**1.0**

The income statement clearly shows strong NBI fluctuation that financial management will seek to reduce with the use of floating/fixed interest rate swaps. Financial management will then be faced with a decision on the inclusion of new loan production to its calculations. A symmetrical decision will then apply to liabilities. After all, current accounts from a legal standpoint are considered to be overnight resources.

Calculating static gap

In static gap analysis, the most common method only inputs the fixed rate stock while creating an amortization convention for current accounts. Let us assume that in order to come closest to its asset, this assumption is an amortization of current accounts also over a 5-year period.

Floating interest rate loans will be included in the gap analysis for the initial year, given that the index is known then.

Table 8: Static interest rate gaps

	initial	yr 1	yr 2	yr 3	yr 4	yr 5
fixed rate stocks	100	80	60	40	20	0
floating rate stocks	100	0	0	0	0	0
fixed rate assets total	200	80	60	40	20	0
amortized current accounts	200	160	120	80	40	0
Resulting STATIC GAP	0	-80	-60	-40	-20	0

On the basis of this measurement and to cancel the "gap", management will need to treat the following fixed rate lender swap program:

- 20 for a 5-year term
- 20 for a 4-year term
- 20 for a 3-year term
- 20 for a 2-year term

After a year, management will adjust its hedging since its balance sheet will have evolved. It will adjust this way every year.

Table 9: Static interest rate gap after 1 year

after 1 year	yr 1	yr 2	yr 3	yr 4	yr 5
fixed rate stocks	100	76	52	28	4
floating rate stocks	100	0	0	0	0
fixed rate assets total	200	76	52	28	4
amortized current accounts	200	160	120	80	40
resulting STATIC GAP	0	-84	-68	-52	-36
already hedged gaps	80	60	40	20	0
gaps to hedge		-24	-28	-32	-36

Dynamic model calculation

In a number of increasing or decreasing interest rate scenarios, the dynamic model directly simulates income statements. We assume here a flat curve that shoots down by 100 bp in Year 1, NBI will drop from 12 to 10.8:

Table 10: Income statement in case of a 100 bp decrease

	initial	yr 1	yr 2	yr 3	yr 4	yr 5
floating rate	6%	5%	5%	5%	5%	5%
Fixed rate	6%	5%	5%	5%	5%	5%
fixed rate loans NBI	6.0	5.8	5.6	5.4	5.2	5.0
stock	6	4.8	3.6	2.4	1.2	0
new production	0	1.0	2.0	3.0	4.0	5.0
floating rate loans NBI	6.0	5.0	5.0	5.0	5.0	5.0
stock	6	4	3	2	1	0
new production	0	1	2	3	4	5
NBI total	12.0	10.8	10.6	10.4	10.2	10.0

The hedging swaps program will have to cancel the decrease in NBI. There should be the following nominal amounts:

Table 11

	initial	yr 1	yr 2	yr 3	yr 4	yr 5
NBI total	12.0	10.8	10.6	10.4	10.2	10.0
new NBI / initial		-1.2	-1.4	-1.6	-1.8	-2.0
Swap hedge nominal amount		120	140	160	180	200

Operationally, financial management will address our sample for a 5-year term:

- 120 for a 5-year term
- 20 for a 4-year term in one year
- 20 for a 3-year term in two years
- 20 for a 2-year term in three years

In real life, it would enter probably into 120 of swaps of duration 5 years, and 20 of forward swaps same duration (5 years) starting year 1, year 2, year 3…. up to 5 years, in order to start covering years after the fifth year. Financial management could also chose the same hedging strategy to the one mentioned in static gap analysis, but it would then take on interest rate risk.

The fact remains that hedging to remove interest rate risk is far more important **here than what was calculated in static gap analysis**.

Comparing the two strategies

Through the dynamic model, one can design hedging that is perfect for the translation of the yield curve. The static gap model on the other hand opens up over time to greater interest rate risk.

Table 12

	initial	yr 1	yr 2	yr 3	yr 4	yr 5
floating rate	6%	5%	5%	5%	5%	5%
Fixed rate	6%	5%	5%	5%	5%	5%
NBI total before hedging	12.0	10.8	10.6	10.4	10.2	10.0
Floating NBI / initial		-1.2	-1.4	-1.6	-1.8	-2.0
NBI static swaps		0.8	0.6	0.4	0.2	
static NBI total	12.0	11.6	11.2	10.8	10.4	10.0
dynamic NBI swaps		1.2	1.4	1.6	1.8	2.0
dynamic NBI total	12.0	12.0	12.0	12.0	12.0	12.0

Note that in this example, potential swaps that were set up after the interest rate shock have no impact: the adjustment during years 2 to the swap portfolio was not taken into account.

We get the same result for other interest rate fluctuation scenarios, even if hedging is not perfect anymore:

Table 13

	initial	yr 1	yr 2	yr 3	yr 4	yr 5	Standard deviation
floating rate	6%	3%	2%	8%	10%	6%	
Fixed rate	6%	5%	4%	9%	5%	7%	
NBI total before hedging	12.0	8.8	7.4	14.4	16.0	12.4	
Floating NBI / initial		-3.2	-4.6	2.4	4.0	0.4	
Static NBI	12.0	11.2	9.8	13.6	15.2	12.4	1.9
Dynamic NBI	12.0	12.4	13.0	11.2	8.8	12.4	1.5

Generally speaking, static gap analysis has some weaknesses that ALM offsets with additional calculations:

1. Structurally, it underestimates the interest rate downside risk to retail banks' balance sheets.

2. It is very sensitive to amortization assumptions for deposit accounts without fixed term. And **these are purely a convention**[21]. In some banks, amortization policies were for a 20 year timeframe, whereas others for very similar client profiles, applied 7-year policies.

Table 14: Gaps' sensitivity to current account amortization conventions

initially	initial	yr 1	yr 2	yr 3	yr 4	yr 5
fixed rate loans inventory	100	80	60	40	20	0
floating rate stocks	100	0	0	0	0	0
fixed rate assets total	200	80	60	40	20	0
current accounts amortized over 10 years	200	180	160	140	120	100
resulting static gap	0	-100	-100	-100	-100	-100
vs. GAP if current account amortised over 5 years	-80	-60	-40	-20	0	-80
vs. GAP if current account amortised over 20 years	-110	-120	-130	-140	-150	-110

In the case of a long-term fixed rate loans portfolio, for instance in the case of lending to local authorities, an amortization convention for current accounts that is too fast can lead to invert interest rate risk. In the following example, the portfolio consists of 20-year linear amortizing loans. During standard activities, it faces trivial downside risk on rates for the production of new loans. If the current accounts amortization policy is less than 20 years, the result will be the opposite:

Table 15

initially	initial	yr 1	yr 2	yr 3	yr 4	yr 5
Fixed-rate loan stock 20 years linear amortizing	200	190.0	180.0	170.0	160.0	150.0
floating rate loan inventory	0	0	0	0	0	0
Total fixed rate assets	200	190.0	180.0	170.0	160.0	150.0
Current accounts amortized over 10 years	200	180	160	140	120	100
resulting static gap	0	10.0	20.0	30.0	40.0	50.0
versus GAP if current account amortized over 5 years		30	60	90	120	150
versus GAP if current account amortized over 20 years		0	0	0	0	0
versus GAP if current account amortized over 30 years		-3.3	-6.7	-10.0	-13.3	-16.7

---

21 See previous paragraph

Generally, for a fixed rate loans portfolio, the static GAP rate depends on the current account amortization convention: if the convention replicates loan amortization, the gap is nill; if amortization is slower, then there is a negative gap and one needs to invest longer-term (that is the real downside risk for rates during a "normal" phase where M1 does not drop). If amortization is faster, the gap becomes positive, wrongly suggesting that the bank is at risk of rising interest rates (we assume a sustainable business configuration).

3. It does not take into account other balance sheet distortions due to an increase in loan production or interest rate indices differences. Management could also fear rather than a simple translation of the yield curve, a flattening or a steepening of the yield curve for instance. By the way this type of risk is central to market refunding banks.

Yet currently static gap analysis is the most popular. There are a number of reasons for this popularity:

- Banks often do not have the adequate software for complex modeling of their balance sheets. Under pressure from regulators, banks are just starting to get those. In large organisations, however, financial directors are unfortunately too detached from their operational role to be sensitive to the importance of these models to support their reflection on their institution's broad balance. But this reflexion is the essence of their role. It ensures the long-term viability of their institution, well ahead of financial communication and prestigious road-shows (that are extremely time consuming).

- ALM teams are often uncomfortable to include new activities that seem random. Furthermore, they lack the means to measure NBI sensitivity to these activities, knowing that loan production is cyclical and therefore also related to interest rates.

- Static gaps were historically the first method used and this developed into a habit, this habit was further endorsed by the regulator.

- It helps to justify short hedging, and as such removes the risk of jeopardising the future (if we take short-term conventions)

- It gives the illusion of automatism in hedging strategies, as the balance sheet decreases over time.

- It allows for controversial swift convention change when rates are low in order to reopen its exposure to rising interest rates ...

Significant challenges are inherent to the global modeling method:

- The first one is technical, because it is complex to model an entire bank balance sheet. It is complex to make sense of all its variables. The trickling down effect of the production of fixed rate loans, which is self-amortizing, is particularly difficult to model.

- Once simulations have been mapped out, the Assets/Liabilities Manager has to decide on a chosen hedging strategy: should he or she hedge over 3, 5 or 20 years? This key issue requires a in-depth explanation (see subsection "Which duration for financial management steering policy ?").

In fact, as mentioned previously, static gap analysis is not based on empirical research on the stability of current accounts. From the perspective of interest rate risk only, the amortization convention on outstanding current accounts turns out to be the target pace at which an interest rate shock gets transferred into the balance sheet. In our simple scenario, it will be gradually spread / transferred over a 5 year period. From an analytical perspective of the bank, looking at the bank from a split or compartmentalised per business unit / core activity perspective, client business bears the brunt of this sensitivity to interest rate risk. If instead of having a 50% floating interest rate loan production in our example, we choose to produce 100% of loans at fixed interest rate, ALM would have had to set up no swap, and the interest rate shock would have gradually spread throughout the balance sheet via client business. In static gap analysis, the choice of amortization convention has first of all a significant impact on how fast is spreading an interest rate shock through the incomes statement. It is also related to management methods that approach the bank analytically from a split or compartmentalised per business unit / core activity perspective (see chapter on NBI analytics and internal rates). This is because it provides an investment benchmark strategy for indefinite-term deposit collection. This relates as well to liquidity issues that are discussed below.

An outdated argument

The argument between proponents of static and dynamic rate gap analysis is indeed slightly outdated and ALM teams must first of all emphasize an approach that is both pragmatic and practical, that allows them to respond quickly to a management that wants to understand the consequences of their chosen financial strategy on their real and complete income statement. If they do not have access to adequate systems, teams must do with what they have access to. If they have access to these means but chose to stick to the traditional "static" gap analysis method, they will need to reconcile both approaches.

Screenshot 10: A sample dynamic analysis indicating monthly fixed rate static gaps estimated for each future year. For comparative purposes, the pop-up indicates the expected annual NBI per scenario with dynamic gap analysis.

Result									
		Opening Balan...	11/2013	12/2013	01/2014	02/2014	03/2014	04/2014	
Tiers 1									
Regulatory Capita								Scenario Comp	
Solvency Ratio or	Report Type:	Annually				Show:	Final		
Solvency Ratio Ti									
Solvency Ratio	Scenario		Opening Balance	11/2013 - 10/2014	11/2014 - 10/2015	11/2015 - 10/2016	11/2016 - 10/2017	11/2017 - 10/2018	
Liquid assets	base			250,430.46	253,153.04	267,281.71	284,024.5	292,351	
L1 Liquid asse	fwd + 100 bp			278,827.34	277,026.2	292,985.22	311,964.79	322,997	
L2 Liquid asse	forward + 200 bp			307,043.48	300,556.21	318,283.82	339,563.59	353,465	
L2A Liqui	forward + 300 bp			334,910.25	323,327.67	342,649.2	366,239.9	383,137	
L2B Liqui	fwd -100 bp			221,869.08	229,040.39	241,383.25	256,058.67	261,92	
Net Cash Outflo									
Cash Outflow									
Cash Inflows		24,569.48	51,825.64	70,060.55	80,638.96	101,535.95	117,811.82	138,879.83	
Liquidity Coverage Ratio		.65	.96	1.03	1.35	1.59	1.78	2.24	
ACTUALIZED GAP 1%		48,980.6	54,349.3	57,607.79	59,485.04	61,293.65	63,024.23	65,392.59	
STATIC GAP / EQUITY		.07	.08	.08	.09	.09	.09	.09	
TOTAL GAP		4,898,059.68	5,434,929.73	5,760,778.97	5,948,503.94	6,129,365.42	6,302,423.34	6,539,258.73	
GAP month 0									
GAP month 1		370,168.42	347,968.23	-1,798,973.54	-1,782,859.74	-1,906,809.82	-1,920,446.4	-1,941,519.41	
GAP month 2		407,119.89	-1,773,969.94	-1,776,458.23	-1,878,731.46	-1,892,408.89	-1,927,690.62	-2,073,644.53	
GAP month 3		435,735.35	-1,745,479.88	-1,767,193.63	-1,864,355.89	-1,889,678.52	-1,909,740.22	-2,055,585.15	
GAP month 4		-1,718,308.87	-1,738,240.53	-1,754,695.35	-1,861,650.87	-1,871,753.53	-1,891,588.87	-2,012,337.72	
GAP month 5		-1,715,094.72	-1,729,767.5	-1,751,859.21	-1,843,751.24	-1,853,627.58	-1,848,279.04	-1,995,898.73	
GAP month 6		-1,785,522.94	-1,809,989.09	-1,817,017.35	-1,825,650.64	-1,810,343.16	-1,831,771.9	-1,987,096.5	
GAP month 7		-1,782,893.68	-1,792,140.01	-1,798,942.06	-1,782,391.58	-1,793,861.42	-1,822,903.49	-1,977,841.4	
GAP month 8		-1,775,069.79	-1,784,089.97	-1,765,708.3	-1,775,935.19	-1,795,018.42	-1,813,565.58	-1,968,422.08	
GAP month 9		-1,893,840.39	-1,877,764.75	-1,886,254.12	-1,904,186.08	-1,922,882.73	-1,941,348.53	-1,958,834.78	

In any case, progress in data base and modeling techniques provides access to highly sophisticated and integrated bank financial management: deposit collection management, capital reinvestment strategy, sensitivity to economic production environments, modeling current and savings accounts, and hedging strategies... From a financial point of view, the bank is a balance sheet that gets distorted over time while journeying through a number of shocks. The report summarizes interest rate, credit, market and liquidity risk. There is a need to comprehensively analyze everything: liquidity risk is primarily reflected with a rise in the cost of money for the bank, credit risk has an impact on results, but also on capital, on liquidity, on deposit collection ... ALM teams must therefore strive to understand the risks that they face in a manner that is global. Another crucial topic is the reinvestment benchmark for current accounts. It is important since it defines liquidity risk profiles and the bank's investment benchmarks. This however does not absolve ALM teams from calculating their overall interest rate risk.

The most surprising dimension of this debate on static and dynamic gaps is that the regulator, quite clearly, considers static methodology as "the simplest technique"[22] while highlighting explicitly its limits[23]. It unquestionably favors dynamic analysis because these more sophisticated techniques allow for dynamic interaction between the financial flows and interest rates, and captures more accurately the impact of implicit securities[24] ».

Given that there is a growing need for forecasts to cover all regulatory ratios (LCR, exchange rate risk…), there is in fact no way around dynamic analysis … The only way to know what a bank's static gaps will be in a year is to use dynamic modeling (the year's production that contributes to stock for use in a year).

On the one hand, from the regulator's perspective, the benefit of static analysis is that it removes the assumption of future production. Applied as a standard, static analysis mitigates the risk of unrealistic assumptions on future production. On the other hand, the predicted estimate of IR sensitivity is often less than the actual one. Above all, by letting banks chose which conventional amortization law to apply, regulatory authorities give them significant independence to manage of their own regulatory ratio[25].

---

[22] Basel Committee on Banking Supervision (2004, p. 27): "The simplest techniques..."
[23] Ibid, p.28 "Although gap analysis is a very commonly used approach to assessing interest rate risk exposure, it has a number of shortcomings…". Given this observation, it is surprising that the known methodological error with regards to conventions is not subject to, at the very least, a certain level of caution.
[24] Ibid, p.30, paragraph 2.15, the regulator is cautious when it comes to regulating sophisticated methods because of the "black box" risk. The issue is that the method used to define the flow rules in static gap is itself by necessity a "black box" when it is not based on the correct reason for using it, or when it is not used wisely, which is still observed too often..
[25] The most problematic is the modification of convention terms: in times of low interest rates, some desks may seek to reverse their positions to lock in a margin to then re-expose themselves after a rise in interest rates. It is then to their advantage to reduce the conventional duration of current accounts amortization. On the

Which duration for financial management steering policy?

Answering this fundamental question for interest rate risk hedging strategy requires to turn to the sources of the profession. A bank is a service industry, intended to provide service to its clients: to provide them with means of payment and treasury and cash-flow management solutions, whether customers are investors or borrowers. Just like all industries that rely on people and systems, banks' organisations and systems cannot be modified overnight. In case the yield-curve collapses to zero, all banks' income statements will deteriorate. The services that they currently provide today in exchange for collecting deposits under market price will need to be invoiced. This scenario, like many others, will adjust over time.

Similarly, the banking business is extremely cyclical since, by definition, banks are there to absorb some of the business cycle shocks (initially via an increase in credit risk). The purpose of ALM is to stabilize the income statement and balance sheet in order to provide management with enough time to adapt to a new operating environment. The duration of its hedging strategies must take into consideration the following two categories of risks:

- a dip in the economic cycle: a recession and exit from recession tends to take around a minimum of 5 years with cycles that seem currently to shorten, beyond the structural impact of globalization on the economic and social model of Western economies.

- a structural change in the operating environment. Currently, a retail banks' outstanding credit is 80% renewed over a 5-7 year period. This seems to be enough time to potentially adapt human resources capacity, to develop new tools and restructure the existing organization. A shorter time span carries greater operational risk. Most of the time, it does not facilitate a return to stability. Here too the Japanese case advocates for a period of 5 to 7 years to allow for the banking product to adjust to the new arrangement. This example is however highly specific and still on going with the abyssal increase in Japanese debt (until the final show-down which appears irremediable without fundamental restructuring). Moreover, it is ill-suited to the European context

contrary, at high interest rates with a steep yield curve, it is in their interest to extend conventions in order to place themselves in a carry position on macro-covering swaps.

of state crisis because of the greater internationalization of national debts which prevents their artificial inflation at zero rates.

Here, as clearly stated by the regulators in Basel III, we get to the core of the steering forecasting function of the financial management: to try to preempt a number of potential scenarios that the bank could face, "including those least likely to occur".

Key decisions that are taken a little too lightly have serious consequences in real life. And we see it today: without getting into savings & loans bankruptcy, the existing low interest rates start spreading across banks' balance sheets. However loan duration and increased margin on new loans' production mitigates the phenomenon and makes it a more gradual process. Brokers are another example of the same effect. They have not had the opportunity to slow down the diffusion of low rates across their balance sheets. Yet most of them had neglected this major structural risk: as they faced a downward trend in their commission fees, the crisis had an impact on three levels. It affected them through a decline in trading, in short-term interest rates and in the spread of short-term government bonds in which they invest their treasury. Few have put in place appropriate interest rate swaps. Today, they have no alternative but to merge or to reposition themselves so as to stabilize their income statements, especially as the regulator is more demanding with regards to capital requirements and to investment policies for client funds, after MF Global filed for bankruptcy (following REFCO's bankruptcy).

Liquidity analysis

If one wants to mark to market current accounts, whether to sell the bank or to organise a transfer price between the Asset Liability and customer collection department, at how much shall they be evaluated? Even if historically, M1 is extremely stable and grows more or less in line over the long-term with the economy, is it reasonable for a bank to consider this resource as permanent and to place it in very long-term investments? Intuitively, caution dictates that certain limits be set with regards to liquidity transformation. Here are a number of reasons for this :

- In case of massive loan losses, the bank will see its capital contract. If it faces at the same time, and due to this, deposit flight, it is likely that its survival will be directly threatened [26].

---

26 Moulin (2008)

- A regulatory change, a systemic crisis can lead to the flight of funds.
- Can a bank afford to block its most valuable asset (because it is stable and free or substantially free presently) in investing heavily it the very long term?

The question of the duration of current accounts is rather the question of their investment: which investment strategy is both acceptable and reasonable? It is common to confuse these two notions. We previously noted that current accounts had very specific characteristics: they can be modelled in stock and grow symbiotically with the economy except in situations of crisis. Yet their investment strategy has never been looked into even though it is not only key to bank liquidity but also key to profitability analysis: what portion of the NBI comes from deposit collection activity, how much comes from loans book activity? This question is more important than it seems. Bank management generally tends to allocate little time and energy to deposit collection (apparently because it carries less risk) when compared to time allocation for credit. Developing a deposits investment strategy also is an opportunity to value them as well as to improve financial analysis of banking business value creation (even if doing so is affected by the links between deposit collection and credit).

For a bank, defining a reasonable and realistic investment deposit strategy actually means defining its target liquidity profile on its portfolio of assets. This goal can only be understood from a time perspective: conventions on the collection of indefinite deposits in static liquidity gaps do not relate to the duration of liabilities but to the duration of the assets in which the liabilities are invested, and not in a static but in a dynamic approach.

Let go back to our previous example, this time from a liquidity angle. We now assume that we have a stable rythm (after year 5) and that the bank produces loans at fixed rate (the rate issue has been fixed earlier, with the portion of it in variable rate no longer necessary) at 5-year amortization. The balance sheet is trivially stable and the bank is required to fund its production of 33.3 together with the leftovers from the year.

Table 16

	initial	yr 1	yr 2	yr 3	yr 4	yr 5
assets	110	110	110	110	110	110
government bonds	10	10	10	10	10	10
credits total	100	100	100	100	100	100
stock	100	66.7	40.0	20.0	6.7	0.0
new production	0	33.3	60.0	80.0	93.3	100.0
stock in terms of time to maturity (linear amortization over 5 years)						
5 years remaining	33.3	33.3	33.3	33.3	33.3	33.3
4 years remaining	26.7	26.7	26.7	26.7	26.7	26.7
3 years remaining	20.0	20.0	20.0	20.0	20.0	20.0
2 years remaining	13.3	13.3	13.3	13.3	13.3	13.3
1 year remaining	6.7	6.7	6.7	6.7	6.7	6.7
liabilities	110	110	110	110	110	110
current accounts	100	100	100	100	100	100
capital	10	10	10	10	10	10
solvency ratio	10%	10%	10%	10%	10%	10%
NSFR	150%	150%	150%	150%	150%	150%

With regards to liquidity, is the situation adequate?

- During "normal" times, times that have no effect on liabilities, the bank credit portfolio is exposed to risk that is supposed to be hedged with capital funds (we assume core equity of 100% with RWA at 100, that is an ESR of 10%). Although every case should be looked at separately, for an adequately diversified and capitalized bank this idiosyncratic credit loss risk remains relatively minor.
- In the event of a liquidity crisis (in case of a systemic crisis), it can slow down the production of new loans to 33.3 and liquidate government bonds[27] to compensate for the flight of deposits.
- Its liquidity position is perfectly stable over time.

---

[27] In order to slow down the flight of deposits, the Bank of Spain made it mandatory during the crisis for banks to declare international transfers above a certain amount. It simultaneously halted price war on term deposits between banks. Both measures were designed to stabilize bank deposits pending the recapitalization of the banking sector.

Clearly, this institution is robust when operating in a low credit risk volatility environment like the Northern Eurozone environment. In applying the NSFR 2010 definition, one gets a 150% ratio. This means that we could technically lend longer and thus capture a little more of the liquidity spread.

To convert these qualitative assessments into a quantitative form, one must model the key variables affecting the bank's balance sheet. What is referred to here is credit loss (PD and LGD), interest rates (because the two are connected) and deposit behavior (growth rate). The model must actually trigger the flight of deposits as soon as loss is high (in the case of an idiosyncratic crisis scenario). The second sensitive scenario is that of a systemic crisis, as in Greece and to a lesser extent in Spain[28], which would trigger a flight of deposits, a decline in production, a rise in claims but also an increase in margins. With this example, we see that a purely quantitative approach is difficult to implement and must be preceded with deterministic scenario simulations to better understand the balance sheet.

About liquidity transformation and targets of runoff

Each department will set a target transformation level that will depend on:
- institutional characteristics and risk aversion,
- liquidity spread, that is a steepening of the yield curve and expectations with respect to this curve[29]. It is also worth noting that positioning based on liquidity spread is often the result of a tactical choice. Strategic choice refers more to decision-making with regards to limits by outstanding market (real estate, public authorities, PPP, utilities …), the characteristics of each of these markets guiding most often granted durations.
- Assets available, especially with respect to their term and liquidity, which once again is a constraint on the asset and not on the liability.

---

[28] In order to slow down the flight of deposits, the Bank of Spain made it mandatory during the crisis for banks to declare international transfers above a certain amount. It simultaneously halted price war on term deposits between banks. Both measures were designed to stabilize bank deposits pending the recapitalization of the banking sector.

[29] Moulin (2012), p.14, sub-section, 1.1.2 *"Courbe des taux, taux forward"*.

Bank liquidity leverage

This concept is little seen in the existing financial literature. It formalises an observation made by many practitioners and by the Basel Committee[30]. Outstanding customer deposits are not subject to the same renewal uncertainties as outstanding market liabilities. In case of difficulties, the latter dry out faster. Outstanding customer loans are connected to the clients' real economic life. This makes them much less sensitive than debt raised in the financial markets: outstanding customer debt is renewed on a more stable and regular basis. Clients are observed to place greater trust in their banks than market actors do. Clients do not use arbitrage between banks in the same country, let alone between countries or geographical areas, as did monetary funds in Europe during the 2008 crisis.

- We call **liquidity leverage** the ratio of customer assets (loans primarily) and other stable assets financed by market resources divided by the total customer resources. Or inversely, the customer collecting surplus over customer assets reinvested on the market, divided by the total customer resources.

- We call the **customers' assets resources ratio** the ratio between the sum of customer assets and other permament assets over the sum of customer resources and equity.

- The term **"banking leverage"** refers to the surplus portion of the market collection that is reinvested in the market based on the total balance (the ratio is also sometimes calculated relative to equity): it is therefore the portion of the financial balance sheet that is independent from bank customer activities. Banks may indeed benefit from their banking licenses and therefore their refinancing capacity in particular at the ECB to carry positions and therefore to increase their NBI. Banking leverage may also exist due to a desire to maintain cash reserve or for other technical needs.

---

30 Basel Committee on Banking Supervision (2011), p.1: "one of the main reasons (why) the economic and financial crisis, which began in 2007, became so severe... was... the excessive on and off-balance sheet leverage".

Table 17

bank	surplus	at equilibrium	deficit
total balance sheet	120	120	120
client deposits and capital funds	100	100	100
customer assets and permanent assets	80	100	110
net to invest (+) or refund (-) on the market	+20	0	-10
liquidity leverage ratio	+20%	0%	-10%
customer asset-resources ratio	80%	100%	110%
banking leverage	17%	17%	8%

These definitions definitely bring up the question of the customer base. A structured loan made by a small mutual bank to a very large firm usually below market conditions artificially inflates customer assets when in reality it is simply a speculative market transaction within banking leverage activities. Time deposit collection on this type of corporate will result in the same volatility as with market resources and does not qualify as customer deposits. The Basel liquidity ratio norms provide rules to facilitate the identification of such errors of allocation. Internally, a responsible financial department and a general management that has integrity should not even face this kind of issue (the production of regulatory statements is another matter altogether as institutions seek to interpret definitions to their advantage, a fact that regulators accept as part of the game, ensuring only that advantageous interpretations stay within the boundaries of what is reasonnable). It is in fact quite the opposite, if the issue arises, it is often that there are fundamental human contributions (see the last part).

One of the bank's financial management strategic choice for the future economic cycle is to set a liquidity leverage target (in general, it is best to have a medium-term goal to ensure that there is enough time to adjust, for instance a 5 years goal). This choice is crucial because it will affect the required credit development level in relation to collection. The two do not develop at the same pace, and overtime the arising difference between the outstanding loans and deposits collection cannot go on indefinitely, as the institution would grow increasingly dependent on the markets and would be irreparably exposed in the case of a crisis to the same end as the one faced by DEXIA.

Of course, there are cyclical market conditions where lending activity is more dynamic than collection. These conditions may explain a temporary gap in the differential between customer collection and loans production. Often it is the balance sheet resulting from the traditional decision to increase market share by using credit as a harpoon to attract customers.

There are also naturally unbalanced markets. This is the case in most countries with well-developed pension funds. This is also the case in France with life insurance and governmental tax free savings accounts. Banks in France are indeed very large life insurance collectors. But these are not visible on balance sheets. Managed directly by the insurance companies, they certainly are reinvested in part into banks, but in much more diverse ways and often beyond the geographical area of the country itself. French insurance companies actually have as their primary assets, not only bank assets but state bonds. They are also fond of corporates bonds, of ABS and potentially also directly credits. In any case insurance operate with limits, some defined by the regulator. This means for example that they cannot have more than 10% reinvested in their collecting bank[31]. In France, life insurance has become essentially a tax shelter and not, from an actuarial approach, an actual life insurance product. This tax benefit artificially magnified outstanding deposits and has led to structurally unbalanced bank balance sheets, all to the detriment of balance sheet deposit collection. There is also the added fact that there has been no innovation in customer collecting bids from the banks over the past twenty years.

In stark contrast, banks in the USA are structurally cash-rich. This is due to the local market culture where loans are sold via securitization and where credit and collections are compartmentalised, effectively managed separately. It should also be noted that this system is no better than the former. Quite the contrary in fact, it facilitated the spread of the subprime crisis to bank balance sheets. Banks actually invested their surplus in RMBS when they had limited credit risk knowledge on those. In this case, banks in the USA bought RMBS subprime. These spread into bank balance sheets, which probably would not have otherwise kept or accepted them.

The imbalance between resources and customer assets is always analyzed with caution, as it can have structural causes or be a thoughtful and measured decision to increase market share. But it is also sometimes a sign of excessive loan production. It is of course easier to grow one's balance sheet through loan production than through deposit collection. The saying that loans make deposit collection is not always correct, especially in France.

---

[31] and the direct acquisition of ABS tranches or credits.

It is a classical trap for banks to inflate their balance sheet through credit. The most typical example was probably with Crédit Lyonnais. In that unfortunate case, the classical and logical corollary was observed, that is a bad loan selection of the biggest files (especially international ones). DEXIA is another example of a bank that has grown primarily through loan production, this time on performing loans, while neglecting issues with collection from clients. Coupled with this, there was a poor appreciation of refinancing risk [32]. The bank found itself far too dependent on markets both at times of market closing and of liquidity repricing. It could not cope. It is worth mentioning that it is extremely difficult to hedge one's own spread risk[33] as an issuer, especially for long maturity terms as DEXIA did with both utilities and its loans to local governments... except by borrowing long-term.

Conversely, a good ratio can also prove to be artificial if for example the bank securitizes a lot. It is important to highlight that some banks include covered bonds issuance in their customer deposits as these issuances are closely linked to their customer business and have always been accepted by the market during the crisis.

What equilibrium level should be sought? Nowadays, the market demands at least a perfect equilibrium between customer assets and market resources, that is to say, a ratio less than or equal to 100%. This balance is difficult to reach in some markets, and particularly in France. Moreover, this equilibrium is not necessarily warranted and further depends on the bank's business mix: a highly focused retail service bank can afford some "leverage" although traditionally this type of bank is in surplus. Quite the opposite in fact, a bank serving major corporates, highly market-focused, relies usually heavily on the market for liquidity and must exert caution because its results are a lot less recurrent and its customer base is way more volatile. Bear Stearns is a typical example of misjudgment of liquidity risk and of overestimating customer deposits stability: deposits were mainly the

---

[32] During the crisis, Dexia had liquidity needs amounting to EUR 50 bn. per day and EUR 250 bn. per month. These are enormous amounts regardless of available collateral.

[33] Buying CDS on its own name leads to counterparty risk on the transaction for the insurer. On the other hand, it is relevant to hedge against market risk together with one's own credit spread risk. In Dexia's case, it would have only provided it some leeway in terms of time, but in the end it was the bank business model that proved to be obsolete.

surplus funds of hedge fund clients in prime brokerage, a deposit resource that has one of the most responsive market behaviors.

The choice of target leverage can be made only after the rigorous and precise analysis of each balance sheet, of customer activity and of the macroeconomic situation. The simulation of every path is required in order to then synthesize the results based on this key target. Its level is as important as the chosen manner of achieving it. Particularly if the ratio is above 100% and that consequently the bank makes use of banking leverage. In this case, the key issue will be to study the refinancing structure: a reasonable use of the market, especially if it is structured with long-term loans and even more via covered bonds issuance, will not jeopardize a financial institution. It is also quite natural in a market where savings are not collected only by banks (see diagram below) and where actually loans are not always generating deposits for banks.

Figure 2

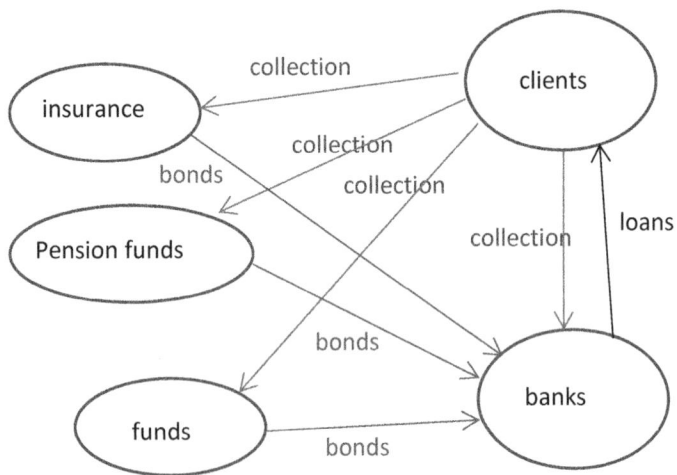

In general terms, this refinancing issue can be represented as follows:

Figure 3

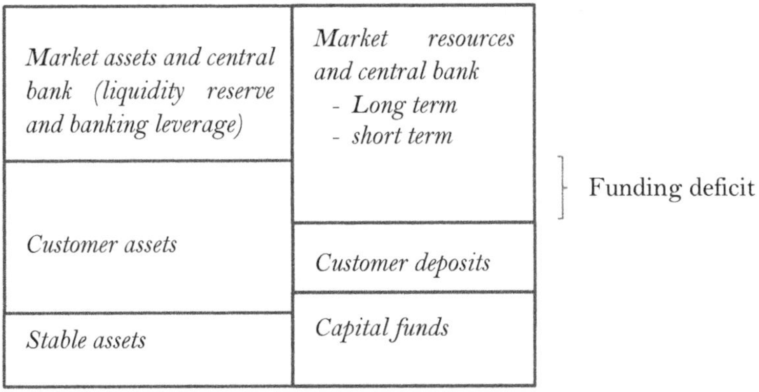

Market assets and central bank (liquidity reserve and banking leverage)	Market resources and central bank - Long term - short term
Customer assets	Customer deposits
Stable assets	Capital funds

} Funding deficit

Banking clients consolidated balance sheet of a country does not necessarily balance out (as in the French case) and can be negative. In this case, the whole system has to make use of the market (funds, insurance companies...) where there are domestic and international investors, or it must reach out to the central bank. Consolidated analysis for each country is interesting as it provides an indication of the average market level on its customer segment.

The bank must find the right balance between the different marketing segments. It must define the level that seems acceptable in terms of deposits and net market resources that it will select for its balance sheet. The choice of liquidity leverage depends on balance sheet growth policy and use of market resources as well as access to the central bank. The central bank is the lender of last resort and ensures during times of crisis the strength of the overall system (provided that in this crisis scenario, bank risk is still acceptable to the central bank).

Banks must thus answer two questions:
- The first one: what level of dependence on the market can I accept? Some very conservative banks have considered that their clients assets must be inferior to their client resources; other, less conservative, or more confident in their access to the market (rating, size, recurrence of results, diversification ...) will tolerate client assets higher than client resources, so refinanced in part by market resources.

- Should these market resources be acquired, the second aspect to consider concerns both its maturity and its type (covered, senior …) so as to avoid jeopardizing the viability of the institution during difficult times. This requires a full balance sheet simulation that takes into account the possibility of accessing the central bank desk. An analysis of deposit stability is also required.

The main error is to first try to borrow as much as possible in covered, then in senior debt, while trying simply to minimize the cost of resources relative to short-term (which in this type of reasoning often takes an excessive share). To reason this way is equivalent to a management opting for a simple opportunistic tactical position without asking the right questions about possible downturn cycles or even the basic macroeconomic situation of the country. This behavior would be obvious to the supervisor who would be entitled to question the added value of such leadership in managing the institution. If we add that this type of reasoning often follows market trends, then it contributes to the herding phenomena that creates speculative bubbles and thus crises, recurrent phenomena in economic cycles.

Taking accounting into consideration

In the major modeling principles, we saw that accounting was the best reference in the face of MtM methodologies that are difficult to understand and that always include several policies. It implies that all modeling must apply the actual accounting rules to the modelisation. One should ensure that what is recorded in cash-flow accounting should be modeled in the same way and that those recorded at market value should be modeled at market value (either through P&L or through equity). Similarly, exchange rates should be identical replicas.

Accounting rules are currently increasing in complexity, as the IASB leads the profession into the "full marked to market" principle, a principle which, as we have seen, is neither necessary nor desirable[34]. This change generates no fundamental conceptual challenges. It just makes programming and simulations heavier.

---

[34] However it will allow some consultants and investment bankers to charge a lot of fees that are unrelated to real benefit to the economy if not for a supposedly enhanced image of reality. It will in any way prove to be false because for most loans, both yield curves and spreads are conventions. This is a fine example of labyrinthine of modern regulation that essentially forgets the essence of the profession. It is right to worry about this unhealthy trend.

Actual difficulty lies more in modeling the monitoring of the result, that is to say the management decision to realize or not any unrealized capital gains, depending on the scenarios: the investment policy of surpluses capital is based on prior experience and expectations of management. However, in banking, it remains a second order effect (which is not the case for insurance).

The connections between different types of risk

Developing different relevant scenarios requires that one takes into account the cross effects between different risks credit, interest rates, liquidity, systemic and commercial risk. These risks can be seen through different key variables of the balance sheet which generally are the:
- yield curve
- bank's spread
- customer margin
- CDR and the LGD rate
- prepayments rate
- inflation
- loan production
- deposit collection progress

The values themselves reflect general economic trends, with three key variables being GDP growth, public sector debt and external balance.

Some links are quite subtle and depend on the economic configuration. For example, higher default rates and lower yield are not always co-dependent in the same proportion. Co-dependent proportionality depends on the origin of the slowdown or its duration. This too is applicable to the relation between decreasing rates and customer margins. Relations must be identified through scenarios, hence the importance of proceeding through stochastic scenarios and also to focus in depth on a few test cases.

Scenarios to consider

Each institution will produce scenarios according to its perspective of risk and of the present situation. Here are the most common scenarios:

Traditional regular flow scenarios

- An economic crisis without an attack on the state debt generally leads to a decrease in the yield curve, an increase in claims, an increase in prepayments, lower inflation, decrease in loan production and according to the origin of the crisis may have an impact on the bank spread and on deposit collection. This often leads to risk repricing, hence to an increase in customer margin. The scope of this type of scenario alternates and speeds at which it unfolds vary, hence the interest of deriving it into several different scenarios.

  A more dangerous crisis situation for the banking sector is a Japanese scenario where the yield curve crashes, where prepayments are on the rise, and where defaults are kept in check. Banks are trying to compensate for lost revenue by increasing loan volume production which pushes margins down. Their liquidity is provided by the central bank and this excess liquidity may result in a real estate bubble. It actually seems that the real estate market in most economies (with the exception of Germany) is affected by a housing shortage. Buyers usually access a maximum monthly reimbursement amount via the bank, they borrow this maximum amount possible depending on the flexibility of the bank in terms of both rates and duration. The price is then adjusted according to the maximum amount of loan available.

  The opposite scenario is a period of economic overheating with credit expansion, rising interest rates, higher production volumes, lower bank spreads, reduced customer margins, reduced claims and a rise in expected inflation. These scenarios tend to be advantageous to banks and the main danger lies in the cyclical downturn that management can foresee for their successors, and which they can neglect. Improvement in activity scenarios may induce a fast reaction by the central bank and not trigger inflation, in this case the impact is only on the variable leg of inflation swaps. These scenarios characterized by a steepening of the yield curve are sensitive to credit portfolio indices (EONIA, E3M set annually or quarterly, averages ...) and should be modeled per type of index.

- A relevant "borderline scenario" nowadays would consist of central banks raising concurrently their inflation target[35] as soon as states manage to balance out their budgets and reduce inflation rate

---

[35] The IMF already brought up this idea. See Blanchard (2010).

sensitivity of their liabilities (mainly pension payments and salary indexation). Indeed such a scenario would then allow for debt burden reduction and would balance out wealth creation between the active and ageing population, in order to reduce the cost of labor and reduce the differential with China. The US will probably be the first to use this tool and Europe will follow for fear of not being competitive.

Run to the bank scenarios

The bank deposits flight scenario is a crisis scenario: the deposits do not erode gradually but react to the risk of loss with flight from the financial institution. Two scenarios can be generally observed: the scenario of a financial institution being stuck in a systemic crisis or the conventional idiosyncratic crisis scenario.

- In the idiosyncratic crisis scenario, the institution suffers loss in one activity: generally in loans or trading loss (fraud, excessive position going in the wrong direction, default on credit risk of excessive size...). In terms of market value, capital funds are severely depleted, the rumor spreads and customers withdraw their money thus accelerating the collapse of the institution. Then the deposit flight rate depends on the type of client: the greater the deposit, the greater the withdrawals; the more financially literate customers are, the faster they will withdraw their money. However, there is always a trigger to a crisis, often initiated by a careless context[36].

A major crisis in the country with a credit crunch and a potential collapse of the currency...

Systemic crisis scenarios for old Europe up to 2008 were observably very theoretical. With the crisis, they have become topical once again. The list of observed country crises on a global scale in recent years is extensive and justifies always considering this scenario: Indonesia in 1998, Turkey in 2001, Argentina in 2002, Iceland in 2009 (assets

---

36 The author observed that accidents do not happen randomly but they always involve institutions that are lax in their management style: risk control failure, governance failure, leadership has little experience in banking and management or is too greedy, there may be overly aggressive refinancing strategy, excessive expansionary credit policy objectives that are incompatible with the institution's capacity...

frozen), Ireland in 2009, Greece in 2010, Spain in 2011, Cyprus in 2013 ... Even if since the Third Republic, due to robust public finances management, the debt crisis was overcome in France, its financial history includes many situations of default[37].

Two types of scenarios can be identified: a destabilizing event (such as the bursting of a bubble, a war, a natural disaster...) and reaching a 'trigger' threshold on state debt. Generally, a crisis combines the two, the first serves as the 'trigger' in a structurally unbalanced situation.

- In terms of speculative bubble, the subprime crisis of 2008 exemplifies the strong connection between a variable, real estate prices and credit portfolio loss rate - for which borrowers had forecast a rise in the value of properties to refinance or to close their operation. A saying goes that "collateral does not ensure credit quality" and in Europe, a collapse in property prices will probably not result in the same downward spiral: insolvency, evictions, foreclosure, falling prices, the collapse of bank balance sheets holding MtM securities via ABS, and the parallel collapse of the construction sector, which drives the rest of the economy into recession. The scenario will be different. The fact remains that the Irish or Spanish examples show that credit offer, property prices and economic growth are connected. In both cases, before the crisis

---

[37] Under Louis XIV, wars already undermined structurally deficient public finances. At the General Assembly, public debt reached 80% of GDP and its servicing absorbed 50% of the state budget. In 1797, the Directoire defaulted on 2/3rd of its debt. The subprime crisis, which has had an impact on France only indirectly, since French banks were able to absorb their own losses, plays a similar role to the American War of Independence on public finances: by cutting tax revenue (initially those coming from banks and then by the companies affected by the crisis) and by inducing an increase in payroll tax, it created huge demand on the state budget which, just as the former King of France, is unable to restructure and preserve its macroeconomic equilibirium. Fortunately, France now benefits from a number of additional safeguards (ECB, euro, IMF, low interest rates, a globalized financial system...) that keep it solvent for now and provide it with leeway to implement these reforms. It is also worth noting from this point of view that the crisis is but a trigger, a trigger that crystallizes a structural imbalance. The government, responding to the fantastic early 2000 financial sector performance, with an inflow of funds that was clearly unsustainable (random banks claimed ROE of over 20% with long-term interest rates nearing 5%), granted financial benefits to a particular section of society (we will not go into the debate on the political legitimacy of these choices which is another subject) in a sustainable and structured manner just as the King did under the former system for the clergy and for nobility. In other instances it set up additional liabilities that are also structural in nature.

and during the bubble, there was observably lax behavior by the banks on lending criteria, banks expended loans duration. During the crisis, both economies experienced a drop in more than 50% of housing prices with a halt to the construction sector (in both cases, it represented between 10% and 20% of economic activity). In Spain, just as in Ireland, the government tried to rescue banks to prevent economic collapse and thus bear most of the losses, with the consequences that this has on its finances and on the growth of the countries (because in the end, one must always pay. Only distribution in time and in the repartition of the loss is altered).

- A crisis on a country's debt has much more serious consequences since it occurs most of the time together with a currency collapse, tension on interest rates or in the case of eurozone countries an explosion in spreads. NPL rates can rise up to 50% or more. Deposit flight occurs fast (for Greece approximately 1% to 2% per month).

Like any systemic risk, a major crisis conducive to a risk of massive withdrawal of funds is unlikely to be mitigated by one single institution, rather it depends on general financial place discipline: any individual protection seems futile in the event of such a large-scale crash. A bank, in the face of such a scenario, must have the primary objective of saving time and of surpassing competitors. One should highlight that this type of situation occurs only in very specific contexts where economic and financial disturbances seem widespread. The essence of LCR regulations heads in this direction since the ratio has the objective of saving time (one month in text) in order to allow the central bank and different states to act. Whereas a local bank can hardly protect itself against a systemic crisis in its zone of coverage, the matter is however clearly one for the executive management of an international group: actually, by going up all the way to the supervision of leading banking groups at the European level, the ECB clearly seeks to distinguish the fate of these major banks from the fate of the states in which they emerged. Monitoring country risk will gradually become global, and executive management will benefit from offsetting business in their historical zone with business in new markets: this is what allowed Santanders and BBVA to withstand the Spanish crisis and even enabled them to support the system by bying off branches from struggling competitors.

About the dialectic between states and banks

The dependence of banks on state debts and thus governments is a topic that can only grow in importance throughout the economic rebalancing between the West and Asia. States are dangerous debtors to banks because although they seem less risky than individuals and corporates, claims they cause are of high magnitude and recovery is almost always beyond the bargaining power of the private creditors, which are subject to state decisions. Yet contrary to university courses taught over the past few years, excessive deficit that is never reduced irrevocably leads to implosion of the financial system. State debt is of course always attractive - no MtM, little or no capital consumption according under Basel II, no loss in stress tests and an almost total refinancing to the ECB - it allows for the creation of NBI simply by using the privilege granted by ECB to banks for refinancing. Generally this banking privilege contributes to inflation by the acquisition of state debt that is refinanced to the ECB rather that by granting loans to the economy, generally through savings, and to a small degree through Central Bank refunding.

Before purchasing government bonds, the key strategic question that a bank must ask relates to the underlying purpose of the transaction. Most banks clearly have no place for funding their government in their business goal. Additionally, in most cases, the underlying motives of such transactions are:

- Either to provide securities to the bank that it can then sell or use as collateral in exchange of liquidity.

- Or for NBI generation when refunding of these securities to the ECB is done on attractive terms. This profit is clearly speculative. In no way can it be compared to revenues generated by commercial activity, even if the assets accepted at the ECB are proportional to business generated, transactions based on state debt are to a lesser degree part of the long-term value of the bank.

- Or it is a customer-oriented market making activity and then the bank must take care of its outstanding stock in relation to its capital.

When a bank takes a position on State debt, even though it is its own sovereign state, it must analyze country risk. Clearly Greek banks were particularly hit by the crisis because they became massive carriers of state debt in order to cash-in spread between government bonds and refunding costs at central bank, in a typical example of adverse selection. Analysis behind this strategy is twofold: increased NBI allows them artificially to survive short-term while credit risks were exploding and in case of default (which was in fact the case), their bankruptcy was becoming a systemic problem. The government also had interests in the short term to encourage this perverse behavior. The only institution that had to and could stop it (it tried to) was the central bank, at the risk of being accused of accelerating the fall of the state. Was the policy of Greek banks intelligence in the long-term? Clearly not. What perspectives do these institutions have for the future? They can only pretend to regain their place as a lender in the economy, which is already a lot if they were able to restore their margins and provide quality service, while waiting to be privatized. At that time, the ECB will benefit from encouraging absorption by European banking leaders to dissociate banking risk from the state itself. For Greece, the situation will be healthier but at the cost of a massive rescue plan which would have been less if these banks had themselves gradually reduced their loans and pushed the state to restructure itself.

For a European country, the Colbertian thesis that one must master its banking sector may be erroneous. It allows the state to access short-term solutions as much by tightening its grip on citizens' savings and "mediating" the ECB as by curbing harmful restructuring on employment in the short-term. However in the long-term, during a crisis, it increases the state's implicit liabilities and removes one of the safeguards against macroeconomic risk of degradation of fundamental financial equilibrium of the state treasury. The case of Belgium, chosing to transfer to a major foreign institution, BNPP, its main national bank, is the first example of this vision. In its wise humility, has the kingdom lost something in the operation? Clearly in case of a financial crisis on the euro zone, it now is in a better situation. As a regulator, all that it would need would be to ensure that the new owner maintains adequate capitalisation. It was a suitable alternative to carrying the risk of rescuing an institution whose total assets exceeded the national GDP. In case of challenges faced in another country, so as to secure citizens' savings, the Belgian central bank will be in a position to block untimely liquidity transfers. From a social point of view, 25% of the BNPP-Fortis capital and 10% of the BNPP parent capital at the time of the transaction were owned by the Belgian state, there was therefore the guarantee that the Belgian entity's integration into the group would not come at the cost of a violent and inopportune job destruction, especially at the height of the financial crisis. By waiving its national entity's international expansion tax benefits, or those same benefits resulting from capital market development, Belgium managed to stabilize its tax revenue while ensuring by backing its bank to a European leader, most likely of higher service quality due to its size and international network. It is also noteworthy that Belgian national debt also benefits from the structural involvement by BNPP, an entity with the capacity to provide, if needed, powerful support given the size of its final balance sheet (EUR 1.907 bn. in 2012 for EUR 376 bn. Belgian GDP and EUR 375 bn. debt).

The building of a unified Europe goes against the very concept of the national champion. The crisis was a prime example of the cost of that strategy at a state level (RBS is one other such great example) and the limited benefits to governments (excluding structural measures implemented as incentives for the financial industry). Institutions having survived without major issues the crisis are either international giants such as BNPP or Santanders or small institutions, mostly cooperative banks.

To end this paragraph, it is important to highlight the connection between the banking industry and governments. Fortunately, management that is of a strong and brave nature allows governments to deleverage. Here too, the case of Belgium shows that debt can be reduced by a percentage of the GDP with thorough work and constancy (debt was thus reduced from 138% of GDP in 1993 to 84% in 2007). The courage of Ireland is another example of restructuring, in this case in the short-term during a major crisis. The IMF, Europe, national institutions have gained considerably in experience with the crisis. With regards to public debt, it is clear that the differentiating factor is a combination of the competency and the will of the management team to restore its equilibrium[38].

Ratios or crisis scenarios: two complementary methods

Sometimes the two approaches of crisis scenario and limits ratio, are presented as mutually exclusive. Both approaches are in fact complementary, both are based on a robust model.

- Ratios are to define operational limits in terms of liquidity and interest rate risk to then be monitored and enforced easily by operators. These limits must be respected at times of normal movement (small-scale).

- More complex to analyse and to monitor, stress scenarios are strategic management of use for the executive management to define ratios.

---

[38] Since The Delian League, the notion that one is to fill-up the treasury for disaster days, wars, or crises, has not been well integrated to pre-emptive measures except by Germany...

Basel committee norms are written in this spirit as they highlight the importance of some ratio [39] providing the minimum ones to abide by (solvency ratio, RSE, NSFR) while highlighting the need for stress tests [40].

Simulations with discretionary or stochastic scenarios?

We have seen the purpose of discretionary scenario analysis to assess the impact of different economic environments on the bank and to gain an in-depth understanding of the mechanisms. Obviously, the danger of such a method is the inability of quantifying the probability on the one hand of the occurrence of such a scenario and on the other hand running the risk of missing out on another type of scenario that is just as dangerous. The Basel Committee recommends that executive management analyses all potential economic scenarios, however unlikely these may be». In this context, it may be helpful to complete the discretionary system with a random scenario generation system. One must highlight as well that regulations developed are more and more in this spirit both in the insurance sector and the banking sector.

In contrast, the random-only scenario-based approach has the disadvantage of quickly evolving into a black box out of which abstract figures are issued (the institution's VaR, the probability of loss on exceptional events, with few data or observations...). Combining the two approaches can, with increased precision, simulate from a core scenario the probability of occurrence of other events. Quite naturally the main difficulty with stochastic simulations is generating random scenarios, especially the generation of correlations. Normal distribution does not take adequately into account those values that are extreme like those observed at times of crisis, but since it is the easiest to use, its popularity is the highest. The second method traditionally in use is the application of observed empirical laws. A third method consists in a combination of the two through the random selection of parameter variations of core empirical scenarios. If on the one hand the method does not provide a way of defining the probability of occurrence of these core

---

[39] Basel Committee on Banking Supervision (2004), p.12: (IV), principle 4, paragraph 36: "Banks should have clearly defined policies and procedures for limiting and controlling interest rate risk"…

[40] *ibid*, p.17 : (V), C, principle 8: "Banks should measure their vulnerability to loss under stressful market conditions - including the breakdown of key assumptions - and consider those results when establishing and reviewing their policies and limits for interest rate risk"…

scenarios, the value of this method is that it enables the generation of groups of related scenarios that have a low probability of occurring, in order to analyse them. The choice of variable is clearly of primordial importance.

What sort of liquidity transformation should one accept?

Stochastic simulations are meant to quantify the probability of default based on random market data behavior assumptions. This means that not only liquidity cost need to be modeled, but more importantly the size of debt that can be sold.

These two variables (cost of liquidity and volume placed on the market) are difficult to estimate: some banks begin these analyses trying to bind their CDS with the quantity of short-term refunding that they were able to raise. Pending a more objective methodology, teams seek to rely on estimates by their treasury experts, on short- and long-term financing terms to define a critical scenario that must be overcome, without being able to give it a probability of occurrence.

Financial management analysis

This entire book advocates a comprehensive approach to prospective financial management for banks from the pragmatic view that an adapted modeling tool should be useful both for ALM and Treasury, for budgeting or for financial analysis. This saves time given that the core of the operational task is there, to present different figures or to bring up balance sheet issues from a global perspective. Since we identified that financial management activity has as its core mission to protect the bank from ALM risk, this activity will generate revenues and expenses that should be monitored and compared to a reference position. Hence it is quite natural to include in the financial activity margins modeling analyse and to mirror it onto customer activities that it is intended to cover. This naturally raises two questions: What are these activities and how to calculate these margins.

Defining analytical activities

The break-down of the NBI per customer type poses no methodological issue if not for the requirement to define an internal rate of return on cash flows between the ALM and business customers. The purpose is to value :

- for a given customer, the margin on the various products and services especially between assets (loans) and liabilities (collection),
- for the overall bank, the share of NBI attributable to the business (collection and loans) and the share due to ALM activity and investment in the capital funds.

Screenshot 11: Allocation of balance sheet items to their analytical categories: the breakdown can be way more detailed per market …

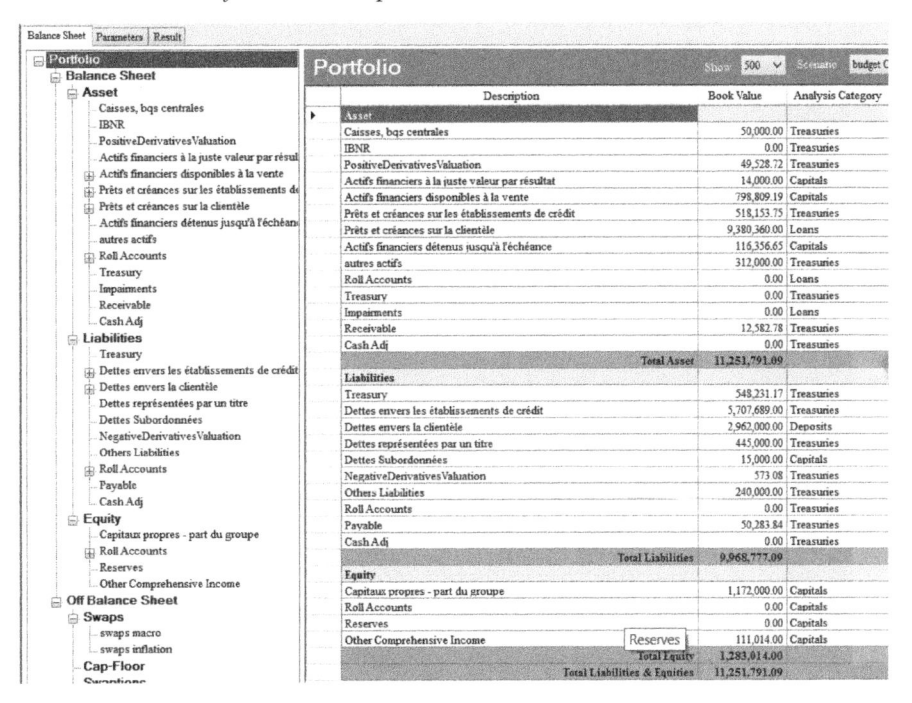

Description	Book Value	Analysis Category
Asset		
Caisses, bqs centrales	50,000.00	Treasuries
IBNR	0.00	Treasuries
PositiveDerivativesValuation	49,528.72	Treasuries
Actifs financiers à la juste valeur par résultat	14,000.00	Capitals
Actifs financiers disponibles à la vente	798,809.19	Capitals
Prêts et créances sur les établissements de crédit	518,153.75	Treasuries
Prêts et créances sur la clientèle	9,380,360.00	Loans
Actifs financiers détenus jusqu'à l'échéance	116,356.65	Capitals
autres actifs	312,000.00	Treasuries
Roll Accounts	0.00	Loans
Treasury	0.00	Treasuries
Impairments	0.00	Loans
Receivable	12,582.78	Treasuries
Cash Adj	0.00	Treasuries
Total Asset	**11,251,791.09**	
Liabilities		
Treasury	548,231.17	Treasuries
Dettes envers les établissements de crédit	5,707,689.00	Treasuries
Dettes envers la clientèle	2,962,000.00	Deposits
Dettes représentées par un titre	445,000.00	Treasuries
Dettes Subordonnées	15,000.00	Capitals
NegativeDerivativesValuation	573.08	Treasuries
Others Liabilities	240,000.00	Treasuries
Roll Accounts	0.00	Treasuries
Payable	50,283.84	Treasuries
Cash Adj	0.00	Treasuries
Total Liabilities	**9,968,777.09**	
Equity		
Capitaux propres - part du groupe	1,172,000.00	Capitals
Roll Accounts	0.00	Capitals
Reserves	0.00	Capitals
Other Comprehensive Income	111,014.00	Capitals
Total Equity	**1,283,014.00**	
Total Liabilities & Equities	**11,251,791.09**	

A brief example is useful to highlight both the scope and process. The Bank is modeled along four lines: two for assets and two for liabilities.

We assume here that loans and collections are matched in terms of duration and of interest rate (in the example the CMS is at 3%). Thus there is no ALM income or fees. Fixed assets are neglected and capital funds are reinvested at 5%.

Table 18

assets	rate	income	liabilities	rate	income

loans	100	CMS+1%	4	deposit collection	100	CMS-1%	-2
investments	10	5%	0.5	capital funds	10	0%	0
		110	4.5			110	-2

NBI analysis across different marketing segments is run using the CMS rate as IRC. Hence we assume that deposit could be reinvested at CMS rate (and therefore for a shorter-term than equity investments) while the credit activity could be refinanced by a loan at CMS (which would cover liquidity cost).

Capital management expenses are neglected: in fact, the cost of financial departments responsible for this activity is marginal compared to the costs associated with customer business (cost incomes ratio assumption at 50%). The cost of risk is fully transferred to the corresponding customer activity. Commissions are allocated at 75% to deposit activity and at 25% to credit activity. The income statement follows:

Table 19 : Incomes statement

Net interest incomes	2.5
Net fees and commissions	1
NBI	**3.5**
General administrative expense	-1.75
Cost of risk	-0.25
Net incomes before tax	**1.5**
ROE before tax	15%
Margin on loan activity	1
Commissions allocated to credit activity	0.25
Cost of risk	-0.25
Net incomes of credit activity	**1**
Profit margin on deposits	1
Commissions on deposits	0.75
Net incomes of deposit activity	**1.75**
NBI from customer deposits net of risk	**2.75**
Administrative expenses	-1.75
Net incomes from customer activity	**1**
Net incomes from equity capital investment	**0.5**

The breakdown indicates that the bank is profitable (ROE before tax is 15%), adequately capitalized, well balanced between credit and collection activities. Knowing that the cost of risk is for the lending business, the primary source of income net of risk is the deposit activity. In reality, it is often the case, and in significant proportions when rates aren't close to zero (because then current account become highly profitable due to their zero interest costs) but banks tend to remain discrete on this matter. It is worth noting that up to the crisis, executive management often neglected collection even though it is a core activity and it is very profitable. The compartmentalisation of fees and commissions between deposit and credit activities is not covered in this book because it is a standard management control matter. Percentages used, however, are realistic enough. The income seems to be made for 1/3rd through the re-investment of capital funds and by 2/3rd through client business. In real life, very similar ratios are observed during normal times (as opposed to times of crisis). In current times, we saw return on equity collapse under the combined effect of lower interest rates and ultra-conservative policies by banks on their own investments. Nevertheless, own funds investment should generally be between 20% and 1/3rd of institutional income (whether they are used for customers' loans or for other investments). Too often, this substantial part of institutional activity lacks both resources and attention from executive management, despite the fact that the amounts at stake are substantial. This notion is all the more important because neither deposits nor loans harmonize in terms of duration and rates.

Now if we develop the above example further, assuming that credit activity should be refinanced at CMS + 0.25% due to liquidity cost while activity collection could be put at CMS - 0.25% (for example, to express a cautious short-term investment). To close up on the banks' NBI, we assume that the two commercial activities deal with the financial department, in exchange for which this one bears the ALM interest rate and liquidity risk.

Hence we have four sources of income and expenses:

- two that are related to client business: deposits and loans,
- two that are related to financial management: ALM and capital fund management.

Income from ALM is of course very sensitive to the chosen internal rate of cession (IRC). In our case, which corresponds to the standard case of a bank in liquidity transformation between collection and loans, ALM results in profit. It can just as much result in loss.

Table 20:

Lending business	
income	4
Internal refinancing costs	-3.25
Commissions allocated to credit activity	0.25
Risk fee	-0.25
Net revenue on credit activity	**0.75**
Collection business	
Internal investment	2.75
Collection fee	-2
Collection commissions	0.75
Collection income	**1.5**
ALM business	
Loan refinancing	3.25
Collection purchases	-2.75
ALM income	**0.5**
Capital funds income	**0.5**
NBI total	**3.25**
Including customer business	2.25
Including financial management	1

We will be quite surprised by the importance of financial management in this analysis. Reality is often far from this observation. We must not however forget that ALM profit is possible only due to client business. Even more given that customer business alone provides access to the central bank and gives access to banking leverage - borrowing on markets or from the central bank.

Internal rates and reinvestment conventions

The IRC corresponds to the rate at which business gets from the division in charge of assets / liabilities the necessary ressources for its lending business. It also corresponds to the rate at which a business reinvests the deposits that it collected from clients. Given that most of the time the two do not share the same characteristics, the business division transfers the transformation risk (the connected rate and liquidity risk) to the asset/liabilities division. This does not mean that the division carries no risk on its business due to market conditions. Rather it means that for each transaction with a known duration, its business margin is fixed (it covers as well for the credit risk).

For transactions of unknown duration, such as current or saving account collections, the system will ensure to a certain degree business margin stability. The rate of cession that is to be applied brings us back to static gap conventions. Indeed the rate corresponds to a reinvestment strategy that is both reasonable and regular. In our case, we had a 5-year linear amortization loan portfolio. If this reinvestment strategy is applied by the ALM, it carries no operational risk with regards to its benchmark (however it still carries a portion of the risk to transaction). This means that the business division carries the risk of interest rate variation. There may be diverging perspectives on this matter, but the fact remains that the general rule is justified. If we take the example of current accounts, with collection for instance at a rate of zero, this kind of deposit does not have the same value if the reinvestment rates are at 14% as in the early 1990s or if they are at 0.17%. On the other hand, defining an internal rate close to the overnight rate with the justification that from a legal standpoint, the current account stock is a day to day deposit does not match the real value of these liabilities. One must also note that the indicated reinvestment benchmark allows for smoothing of the commercial margin: indeed in our example, the reinvestment notional portfolio should amortize by one fifth each year and will thus average the benchmark IRC. It captures the overall liquidity spread. This is in stark contrast to a benchmark that would, for instance, consist of the average of instantaneous 1- to 5-year interest rates).

The rates of cession must take into account the fact that it is the ALM's duty to cover certain risk:

- uncertainty of deposit collection risk
- prepayment risk

ALM is in charge of liquidity management and has access to tools and expertise to manage this type of uncertainty.

Should the ALM carry these risks, it can price them in internal rates on the condition that it respects certain rules. These rules are issued out of its business support role and out of its role as a guarantor of the split between the major revenue drivers:

- ALM cannot price options by assuming that each client is a rational actor. It must take into account statistical risk. With regards to major clients, however, pricing is made line by line, quite naturally.

- ALM must provide rates that are as stable as they can be for business. This implies that it must define reinvestment strategies for deposits of undefined long-term duration. And in doing so, it must take into account the effects of individual behavior (this impact may be managed in a direct manner).

- ALM must support commercial activity by providing it with competitive market rates. At normal times, this is not an issue. But in times of crisis, if the bank spread goes violently away from the market average, decision with regards to the stopping of commercial activity becomes strategic. It is a decision that must be taken after an overall analysis of the situation. Hence there isn't one single rule. Rather, it is the maturity and the competence of financial management that will dictate the behavior that is to be adopted.

- ALM must be vigilant so as not to sponsor a particular type of business, especially those business activities falsely called arbitrage (cash and carry, structured books, market making). These are in fact carry positions. Their "daily" refinancing is but an illusion. In real life, books are never sold (their size render them illiquid, and their sale would generate high loss). Desks borrow the same amounts daily (generally close to their limit). Treasury in this case must invoice a spread to readjust the margin: cash and carry thus often consists of a collateral loan. The price must in theory be such that the choice between liquidation and carrying the position remains [41].

---

[41] This matter is at the core of loss by UBS as described in its well-known report on the origins of its 2008 subprime desk loss.

For ALM, defining IRC has the effect of defining a benchmark hedging strategy: we saw that interest rate risk is permanently diffused in the balance sheet as the stock is being renewed. The only purpose of hedging operations is to even out cyclical risk, and to give commercial activity enough time to adapt. The bank, by defining a targeted indefinite maturity reinvestment strategy for collections, sets the pace at which it is capable of absorbing as a target strategy the real adverse interest rate movement. If management estimates that it needs more or less time, it remains free to move away from this benchmark. It is but a simple benchmark. In our case, it resulted in taking no hedging position and in accepting the progressive diffusion of a translation of the rate curve over the next 5 years. Management would have preferred not to be affected by movement ahead of the 5-year timeline. In that case it would have defined a benchmark that would take into account a current account stock "that is stable over 5 years" and that is then amortized. In actual fact, this latest reinvestment model must be built with existing market instruments: if those do not provide the desired profile, ALM has to constantly adjust its position to prolong its portfolio duration. This can be an operational issue. ALM departments seek consistant strategies which can be modeled.

Investment and benchmark strategy

A collection investment strategy of indefinite duration is equivalent to defining the quantity $q(t)$ and the type of asset $P(t_0, t, T)$ to purchase (with t as date, t_0 initial asset date and T as time before asset expiry). The stock generating income is therefore:

Formula 14: stock generating income

$$Stock(t) = \int_{-\infty}^{t} q(u).P(t,u,T_u).du$$

$$\frac{dStock(t)}{dt} = q(t).P(t,t,T_t) + \int_{-\infty}^{t} q(u).\frac{\partial P(t,u,T_u)}{\partial t}.du$$

In fact, we want the investment policy to maintain constant stock with a buying quantity q hence the following constraint on the price of assets purchased:

Formula 15 : constraint on the price of assets purchased

$$P(t,t,T_t) = -\int_{-\infty}^{t} \frac{\partial P(t,u,T_u)}{\partial t}.du$$

Given that we usually buy at par (if not, we can simply adjust the actuarial rate):

Formula 16

$$\int_{-\infty}^{t} \frac{\partial P(t,u,T_u)}{\partial t}.du = -1$$

If we seek homogeneous assets, and therefore keep T constant, we get:

Formula 17

$$\int_{t-T}^{t} \frac{\partial P(t,u,T)}{\partial t}.du = -1$$

We are interested in this general equation for those assets that are booked at amortized cost regardless of market conditions at time t. $P(t,u,T)$ corresponds in this instance to the outstanding capital funds on t for acquisition u of duration T. We now refer to it as $CRD(t,u,T)$.

Formula 18

$$\int_{t-T}^{t} \frac{\partial CRD(t,u,T)}{\partial t}.du = -1$$

We see that an amortization profile is <u>homogeneous</u> if it only depends on its maturity, that is to say:

Formula 19:

$$CRD(t,u,T) = CRD\left(\underbrace{u-t}_{age}, \underbrace{T}_{duration}\right)$$

The equation is then always respected:

Formula 20 :

$$\int_{0}^{T} \frac{\partial CRD(u,T)}{\partial u}.du = CRD(T) - CRD(0) = -1$$

Amortization functions generally only depend on product maturity (it is not the case for a number of variable rate profiles that depend on past rates) and that respect the constraint: any conventional homogeneous amortization profile is an adequate strategy for current accounts of indefinite term to be reinvested. Let us refer to the most conventional one: a copy of a linear stock amortization (or by steps) by treating as in our example every year the same amount of swap 5 years.

Is there a strategy that is more appropriate than another? In the spirit of static gap analysis, financial literature focuses on amortization dated t of a $Stock_0(t)$ built at time 0:

Formula 21

$$Stock_0(t) = \int_0^{T-t} CRD_T(u).du$$

- In the case of production of bullet loans, CRD(t)=1 for t <T, we obtain linear stock amortization:

Formula 22

$$Stock_0(t) = \frac{T-t}{T}.1_{t<T}$$. This is the conventional renewal stock swap strategy.

- In the case of loan production that amortizes linearly, such as

Formula 23

$$CRD(t) = \frac{T-t}{T}.1_{t<T}$$ we get a stock that has a parabolic amortization profile:

Formula 24

$$Stock_0(t) = \left(\frac{T-t}{T}\right)^2.1_{t<T}$$

- The most interesting (and most elegant) case is that of exponential homogeneous amortization flow. In this case and only in this case, the amortization of the stock and the amortization of the new production are directly proportional. With constant λ, we have:

Formula 25

$$CRD(t) = e^{-\lambda.t} \Rightarrow stock_0(t) = \int_{-\infty}^{0} e^{-\lambda.(t-u)}.du = \frac{e^{-\lambda.t}}{\lambda}$$

Due to this property, this type of amortization profile is often used to model current accounts.

- We have already studied amortization by monthly installments.

Internal rates in practice

The analytical financial analysis implementation challenge is connected to:

- The orderliness of databases to which then the internal rate calculation is to be added. This issue is actually generalized to the entire ALM model and the "IRC" must obviously be either able to be filled or to be supplied evenly afterwards in a homogeneous manner (by distinguishing between fixed and variable rates, capped ...),

- The methodology for determining internal rates: again, the first difficulty is not one that is conceptual, but one that is practical because it requires a consistant and systematic approach.

Screenshot 12 : The IRC ("Internal Rate of Cession") is simply an additional parameter to include.

IE	Finan. Type	Description	Durn	Expiration Date	Coupon	Coupo Type	Fixing Type	Coupon Basis	Freque	Tax	Attrib	CPR	CDR	LGD	Recovery Lag	Currency	Basel	RWA	IRC
A	Fixe...	Entreprises TF...	146	0.04148...	Fixed	In Ad...	A30360	Mon...	Normal	In Balan...	coefRA*...	cdr_corp...	0.75	€	1	100,000.00	0.02
A	Fixe...	Entreprises TF...	145	0.04113...	Fixed	In Ad...	A30360	Mon...	Normal	In Balan...	coefRA*...	cdr_corp...	0.75	€	1	10,000.00	0.02
A	Fixe...	Entreprises TF...	73	0.03313...	Fixed	In Ad...	A30360	Mon...	Normal	In Balan...	coefRA*...	cdr_corp...	0.75	€	1	20,000.00	0.05
A	Vari...	Entreprises T r...	180		E3M	Floa...	In Ad...	ACT...	Mon...	Normal	In Balan...	coefRA*...	cdr_corp...	0.75	€	1	50,000.00	E3M+1%
A	Vari...	Entreprises T r...	96		E3M	Floa...	In Ad...	ACT...	Mon...	Normal	In Balan...	coefRA*...	cdr_corp...	0.75	€	1	2,000.00	E3M+1%
A	Vari...	Entreprises T r...	120		E3M	Floa...	In Ad...	ACT...	Mon...	Normal	In Balan...	coefRA*...	cdr_corp...	0.75	€	1	3,000.00	E3M+1%
A	Vari...	Entreprises TV...	102		E3M	Floa...	In Ad...	ACT...	Mon...	Normal	In Balan...	coefRA*...	cdr_corp...	0.75	€	1	250,000.00	E3M+1%
A	Vari...	Entreprises TV...	123		E3M	Floa...	In Ad...	ACT...	Quar...	Normal	In Balan...	coefRA*...	cdr_corp...	0.75	€	1	450,000.00	E3M+1%
A	Vari...	Entreprises TV...	160		E3M	Floa...	In Ad...	ACT...	Quar...	Normal	In Balan...	coefRA*...	cdr_corp...	0.75	€	1	400,000.00	E3M+1%
A	Vari...	Entreprises TV...	197		E3M	Floa...	In Ad...	ACT...	Quar...	Normal	In Balan...	coefRA*...	cdr_corp...	0.75	€	1	300,000.00	E3M+1%
A	Vari...	Entreprises TV...	135		E3M	Floa...	In Ad...	ACT...	Mon...	Normal	In Balan...	coefRA*...	cdr_corp...	0.75	€	1	50,000.00	E3M+1%
		TOTAL (€)																2,015,000.00	

Product analyses are therefore often less useful than those done by client and branch. The latter can give heterogeneous results, especially when crossed with capital used in each activity.

Screenshot 13 : The IRC analyses are part of the overall analysis, aligned to the principle of unicity. Dividends from participation investments are included in the income category referred to as 'capital'

Result	Opening Balan...	07/2011 - 06/2...	07/2012 - 06/2...	07/2013 - 06/2...	07/2014 - 06/2...	07/2015 - 06/2...
Book Values - Asset	11,251,791.09	11,195,515.56	11,146,337.59	11,101,778.34	11,167,986.19	11,240,905.12
Book Values - Liabilities...	11,251,791.09	11,195,515.56	11,146,337.59	11,101,778.34	11,167,986.19	11,240,905.12
Interest Income - Asset		273,512.9	260,816.52	263,705.21	276,708.76	295,847.15
Interest Expenses - Liabil...		147,910.47	135,371.67	132,599.95	138,075.04	145,274.18
Net Interest Income		125,602.43	125,444.84	131,105.26	138,633.72	150,572.97
Net Interest & Div Analys...		135,754.93	135,604.03	141,250.77	148,786.22	160,725.47
[Default]						
Capitals		8,217.14	7,798.61	6,399.46	3,750.54	227.58
Deposits		44,354.1	43,561.06	43,472.17	43,294.63	43,138.4
Loans		94,803.76	80,902.19	73,052.53	66,921.42	59,701.77
Treasuries		-11,620.06	3,342.48	18,326.61	34,819.63	57,657.64
Gain/Losses on Financial...		11,274.4	11,381.45	11,454.04	11,530.09	11,595.7
Deficit E/A		5,377.82	7,728.99	2,437	2,153	702
commissions		151,560	154,440	157,320	160,200	163,080
Commissions & Others		156,937.82	160,168.99	159,757	162,353	163,782
Net Banking Income		293,814.66	298,995.28	302,316.31	312,516.81	325,950.71
Cost insurance						
charges		-144,780	-146,220	-147,660	-149,100	-150,540
Cost		-144,780	-146,220	-147,660	-149,100	-150,540
Income before impairmen...		149,034.66	152,775.28	154,656.31	163,416.81	175,410.71
Impairment Charge		-20,851.81	-22,736.15	-24,043.75	-24,431.62	-24,855.99
Income Pre Tax		128,182.85	130,039.14	130,612.56	138,985.19	150,554.71
Income tax benefit / (expe...		-43,582.17	-44,213.31	-44,408.27	-47,254.96	-51,188.6
Net Income		84,600.68	85,825.83	86,204.29	91,730.22	99,366.11

For ALM, it is important to distinguish between its various purposes:

- measuring the overall risk of an economic scenario, which requires taking into account the new production of loans and includes the interest rate risk remaining in business activity as well as that inherent to ALM.

- measuring actions to take in order to respect (1) target diffusion pace of a movement of interest rate into the incomes statement and (2) the bank's liquidity target, which is instantly calculated daily depending on the stock.

- And sometimes managing its own capital funds / or proprietary trading.

Rate and volume effect

One of the foundations of NBI analysis is the separation between the impact of interest rate, the volume effect and the cross effect. Even though the following is basic knowledge, it is worth reminding that:

Formula 26:

$$(V + dV).(P + dP) = V.P + V.dP + P.dV + dP.dV$$

Final value = initial value + var. price + var. vol. + cross effect

The intermediation margin is distorted under these two effects: changes in volume as well as variation margins and scenarios have to be quantified while differentiating one from the other. Hence the need to carry out a series of constant volume models as a reference benchmark.

Valuation of deposit collection and loans

Returning to our previous example (first example in the paragraph "definition of analytical activities"), we will now value the collecting and credit compartments separately. For this, we allocate to each of these compartments capital funds that would be required for it to function independently:

- for loans, these are the real capital funds required for the portfolio to meet the SCR (we take a 10% assumption for 100 RWA),
- for deposit collection, one must allocate notional capital, that is to say, as we would need it if we applied the CMS reinvestment strategy to a safe and liquid portfolio of assets. It is assumed that the portfolio would have RWA of 50.

Both capital portfolios are supposed to generate the same return as in our example, which is 5% return. Expenses are allocated to each sub-fund in proportion to their respective NBI (this is a policy).

Lending business is analyzed in three parts:

1. It requires capital, here 10, which will generate revenue (here by 0.5).
2. It consists of a credit stock created by the bank as an industrial tool (its sales teams, credit analysis teams, branches and capacity of selection of customers and files) that already has outstanding future margins to reach, which is referred to in the insurance sector as VIF ("Value in Force"): this is the discounted sum of future margins after charges and risk costs that will be made by carrying the portfolio (in "run-off") and by refinancing it at IRC. In our example, since the activity generates 0.36 outside of equity on a 5-year linear amortization portfolio that is with a modified duration of 2.8 the VIF is measured at 1.02.
3. It carries an intangible value: the bank's ability to generate new loan production yearly, with equal margins.

Collection business can be analyzed similarly, in two parts:

1. Regulatory capital own funds to cover the risks associated with the reinvestment of deposit, in a manner that is both adequate and cautious. Indeed, the deposit activity is also a banking one and we can reason in a fragmented banking model by taking into account the consumption of capital that is connected to the reinvestment of funds. Here we assumed a RWA portfolio at 50%.
2. A goodwill related to the value of this deposit outside the capital.

For a bank listed on the stock exchange, we have market indication of its overall value which corresponds to the value of capital, to the gains or losses on the balance sheet, and to the VIF on the credit portfolio and goodwill / negative goodwill on its business activity.

Table 21

	loans	deposits	total
outstanding	100	100	100
Basel II weights	100%	50%	100%
Notional RWA	100	50	100
Notional capital funds	10.0	5.0	10
NBI	1	1.75	2.75
charges	-0.64	-1.11	-1.75
Incomes out of capital reinvestment	0.36	0.64	1.00
Capital reinvestment return	0.50	0.25	0.50
Net income	0.86	0.89	1.50
ROE before tax	8.6%	17.7%	15.0%
SCR	10.0%	10.0%	10.0%
Modified duration portfolio	2.80		
PER	13.25	6.35	8
Notional capital value	11.4	5.6	12.0
VIF	1.02		1.02
Goodwill	0.36	0.62	0.98
Vif+goodwill	1.38	0.62	2.00
P/BV	1.14	1.12	1.20

In the example above, which corresponds to the case of a profitable bank, quite standard, we dissect this overall goodwill in proportion to the income outside capital funds and across both loans and collections. However this policy is arbitrary and other methodologies may lead to different results. The two activities are closely linked since the same teams work both on loans and collection. Nevertheless the analysis is instructive :

- The ROE from collection business is important eventhough this result is sensitive to the choice of investment portfolio (RWA and yield).
- Most of the goodwill comes from the deposit collection activity. Income is obviously also sensitive to market conditions but in a highly competitive environment with regards to credit (and therefore reduced margins and close to loans and bonds) and restrictions on the deposits, we can understand that this value is higher than the one induced by the bank's ability to generate loans.
- The concept of VIF allows for the reduction of goodwill (VIF is amortized over time while according to the IFRS, a goodwill is simply an "expert" analysis). The model assumes that deposits are invested in assets and loans of like-term.
- In real life, the reinvestment benchmark for deposits is often longer and therefore return is higher.

Overall, it is clear that the bank in this example is undervalued by the market and a prospective purchaser, if he is able to perform more synergies reasonably shall offer a premium. This model also makes it possible to provide the valuation sensitivities of banks to market conditions, an element that is inadequately addressed by traditional analysis. Thus, in our example, the P/BV of deposit collection activity is the element that is most sensitive to changes in market conditions. In real life, the impact is amplified by the fact that the amount of collected deposits itself is directly affected by the interest rate levels (in the example, the assumption is that of a constant deposit amount). The example also highlights the danger with reasoning only in terms of PER for a bank: depending on market conditions, with the same characteristics, goodwills vary tremendously.

Table 22 : Sensitivity of the valuations of the deposit collection activity - PER = 8

Return on capital funds investment	3%	5%	7%	9%
Net income	1.3	1.5	1.7	1.9
Goodwill	-0.62	0.98	2.58	4.18
P/BV loans	1.08	1.14	1.2	1.25
P/BV collection	0.92	1.12	1.33	1.53
P/BV bank	1.04	1.2	1.36	1.52

The sensitivity of goodwill to PER, especially on collection activity makes it a characteristic that is little suited to the valuation of banks.

Table 23

Bank PER	6	8	10	12	15
P/BV loans	1.03	1.14	1.25	1.36	1.52
P/BV collection	0.74	1.12	1.51	1.89	2.46
P/BV bank	0.9	1.2	1.5	1.8	2.25

The ROE business and the ratio of paid goodwill and annual return are more suitable for assessing the profitability of a banking investment.

Table 24

Bank P/BV	0.9	1	1.2	1.5	2
Goodwill/annual incomes	-135%	-68%	265%	1.36	599%
- loans	-85%	-43%	41%	168%	378%
- deposit collection	-145%	-73%	70%	286%	645%

Ultimately, the decision to purchase is extremely sensitive to the price paid because of the bank leverage effect. The basic analysis often presented before the crisis to justify operations is clearly inadequate, and we must go into the details of the constitution of the bank income to be able to understand what we pay and what can be expected from our investment.

For banks that have a valuation lower than net assets, this methodology is used to distinguish what comes from unrealized loss on portfolios of negative VIF or negative goodwill due to insufficient profitability potential. But the two do not have the same value in an acquisition decision: a clearly identified run-off portfolio can always be sold or reserved, a negative VIF may be due to past mismanagement, whereas a negative goodwill is most often the result of structural problems that require managerial measures by definition that are more uncertain in terms of timing and results.

Limits of the analysis

IRC analysis detail the NBI of a client per product and in real life, from collection business and loan business which are intrinsically connected and are there essentially to answer to the needs of the client. These requirements depend primarily on the customer's economic state: the acquisition phase, the savings phase ... A client does not generate consistent profitability and banking relationship can be envisaged only in the long term and in trust.

IRC analysis highlights the financial importance of collection in terms of NBI, of profitability and of liquidity. They are used to catch the attention of management on unhealthy situations (such as savings accounts paid above the replacement cost) and rebalance activity between collection and credit. However, we must avoid any hasty or radical decision that would jeopardize the true source of goodwill of a bank, which is its customers.

REGULATIONS

Banking business is highly regulated. This regulation is reinforced and in recent years has evolved tremendously. It is an ongoing trend and it makes sense as soon as we model the overall balance sheet in order to add the different measurement ratios, given that they represent little additional information.

Screenshot 14: Modeling should include regulatory parameters, relatively simple to recover

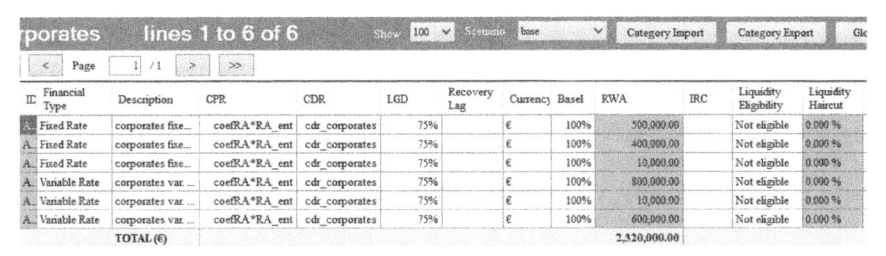

ID	Financial Type	Description	CPR	CDR	LGD	Recovery Lag	Currency	Basel	RWA	IRC	Liquidity Eligibility	Liquidity Haircut
	Fixed Rate	corporates fixe...	coefRA*RA_ent	cdr_corporates	75%		€	100%	500,000.00		Not eligible	0.000 %
A.	Fixed Rate	corporates fixe...	coefRA*RA_ent	cdr_corporates	75%		€	100%	400,000.00		Not eligible	0.000 %
A.	Fixed Rate	corporates fixe...	coefRA*RA_ent	cdr_corporates	75%		€	100%	10,000.00		Not eligible	0.000 %
A.	Variable Rate	corporates var...	coefRA*RA_ent	cdr_corporates	75%		€	100%	800,000.00		Not eligible	0.000 %
A.	Variable Rate	corporates var...	coefRA*RA_ent	cdr_corporates	75%		€	100%	10,000.00		Not eligible	0.000 %
A.	Variable Rate	corporates var...	coefRA*RA_ent	cdr_corporates	75%		€	100%	600,000.00		Not eligible	0.000 %
		TOTAL (€)							2,320,000.00			

The benefits of overall modeling is then to be able to simulate these ratios per scenario in the simulation horizon.

Screenshot 15: Sample end-of-year output that incorporates RSE ratios, LCR and static gaps

	Opening Balan...	11/2013 - 10/2...	11/2014 - 10/2...	11/2015 - 10/2...
RWA	4,482,500	4,536,460.06	4,606,104.11	4,800,260.81
Core Equity	672,000	725,131.45	764,305.43	810,335.48
Tiers 1	672,000	725,131.45	764,305.43	810,335.48
Regulatory Capital	672,000	725,131.45	764,305.43	810,335.48
Solvency Ratio on Core E...	14.99 %	15.98 %	16.59 %	16.88 %
Solvency Ratio Tiers 1	14.99 %	15.98 %	16.59 %	16.88 %
Solvency Ratio	14.99 %	15.98 %	16.59 %	16.88 %
Liquid assets	269,250	260,000	250,750	241,500
L1 Liquid assets	180,000	175,000	170,000	165,000
L2 Liquid assets	89,250	85,000	80,750	76,500
Net Cash Outflows	414,930.52	64,745.8	64,678.37	64,685.06
Liquidity Coverage Ratio	.65	4.02	3.88	3.73
ACTUALIZED GAP 1%	48,980.6	62,806.95	74,932.98	70,039.62
STATIC GAP / EQUITY	.07	.09	.1	.09
TOTAL GAP	4,898,059.68	6,280,695.38	7,493,298.05	7,003,962.02
GAP month 0				
GAP month 1	370,168.42	-2,133,331.25	-1,291,718.01	-1,215,975.8

Interest rate risk

The July 2004 Basel text

Various national regulations are based on the Basel Committee's July 2004[42] text: Principles for the Management and Supervision of Interest Rate Risk. It should be noted today that the interest rate risk is part of pillar II and is therefore not included in the ratio of pillar I [43].

Paragraph 12 of the July 2004 text defines the two most common perspectives for assessing the risk of an adverse movement in interest rates:

- The impact on the short- and medium-term (principle 18),
- The effect on the economic value of the institution that the regulator defines as the net present value of future cash flows (paragraph 20). The discount factor has remained within a broad definition ("discounted to reflect market rate") which provides flexibility on the potential risk premium charged as part of an approach in DDM[44]. The regulator favors this approach (paragraph 21) because the effects of diffusion of an interest rate shock in the balance sheet, as we have seen, are slow and gradual. The effect on two or three years can only incorporate a small portion of the institutions' loss in value.

In fact the text asked to perform both (paragraph 79 b) and provides a ratio to be respected at principle 7: no decrease in economic value of capital funds (tier 1 and tier 2) of over 20% at an interest rate shock defines (paragraph 81) as a translation of +/- 200 bp of the curve or the 1st and 99th percentiles of annual movements observed over a period of 5 years.

Overall risks are listed: risk of translation of the curve, distortion of the curve, basis risks, risks associated with embedded options (paragraph A-16) as well as balance sheet renewal risk ("repricing risk" - A-13) for both assets and liabilities. Thus the regulator explicitly mentions risk related to the new business of loan production.

The approach of the regulator is also global because it includes commissions (paragraph 19) and other income that is sensitive to changes in the economic situation without being part of the interest margin. The regulator also

---

[42] Basel Committee on Banking Supervision (2004)
[43] there are ongoing discussions to incorporate it.
[44] Moulin (2012, p.38), Dividend Discount Model.

mentions that all products and lines of business must be included (paragraph 42).

Finally, the text requires a number of standard rules of measurement, control, information transparency, to the point of recommending an independent review and evaluation of the system (principle 10). This recommendation is now being applied to banks through their internal control department but could lead to a greater requirement with, just as for accounting or for insurance mathematical reserves in some countries, the control through independent external specialized teams (a solution that is nowadays accepted by the regulator, paragraph 68).

The regulatory authorities also clearly places the ultimate responsibility on the board that they want to be informed (Title III Principle 1), accountable for the institution, to fix methods and limits. The board is also entrusted with the responsibility to appreciate[45] the technical capacity of general management for financial products and complex financial techniques.

General management, logically, is responsible for the implementation and daily monitoring of systems and teams in charge of interest rate risk control measure. General management is also responsible for the level of competence of these teams. The new products must be subject to rigorous analysis from an ALM perspective (principle 5).

From a methodological point of view, the static gap method is considered to be one of the simplest (paragraph 45). It is accepted as such despite explicit mention of its weaknesses (Annex I - A repricing schedule). More accurate methods are encouraged and (paragraph 47) the regulatory authorities express their preference for dynamic gap analysis: "these more sophisticated technologies allow for dynamic interaction of payments streams and interest rates, and better capture the effect of embedded or explicit options». Yet it clearly rejects the "black boxes" (paragraph 51) that have been part of the profession for years. Any method should be based on a rigorous approach and approximations must be justified (paragraph 48-50, this implicitly validates their rational use). Management must consider a wide set of scenarios and possibly rely on stochastic generators.

---

[45] It is clear that there was no such accountability for financial institutions during the 2008-2011 crisis.

The standard method for calculating interest rate risk

Appendix 4 provides an explicit methodology for determining compliance with the 20% limit. Here we suggest a mathematical formulation:

- We note $t_1 \ldots t_n$ as the different deadlines (potentially pooled),
- A_i and P_i are the sum of outstanding assets and liabilities (at book value) at fixed rate of remaining time equal to t_i, the difference ($A_i - P_i$) must, if negative, either be reinvested at the current interest rate, if it is positive, it must be refinanced at the same interest rate. Derivatives are added to these elements on the basis of their nominal amount.
- Assets with no maturity are amortized based on convention.
- s_i is the sensitivity (modified duration) of the zero-coupon of term t_i.

We must have:

Formula 27

$$\pm 2\% . \sum_i s_i . \left(A_i - P_i \right) \leq 20\%. \text{ capital}$$

Many assets are not bullet bonds, the formula amounts to calculating the sensitivity of all lines thus summarizing the income statement. The regulators supply for instance a chart of the accepted intervals and their weight:

Table 25

time band	middle of time band (0)	proxy of modified duration (1)	change in yield (2)	weight (1)*(2)
< 1 month	1/24	0.04	2%	0.08%
1 to 3 months	1/6	0.16	2%	0.32%
3 to 6 months	3/8	0.36	2%	0.72%
6 to 12 months	3/4	0.71	2%	1.42%
1 to 2 y.	1.5	1.38	2%	2.76%
2 to 3 y.	2.5	2.25	2%	4.50%
3 to 4 y.	3.5	3.07	2%	6.14%
4 to 5 y.	4.5	3.85	2%	7.70%
5 to 7 y.	6	5.08	2%	10.16%
7 to 10 y.	8.5	6.63	2%	13.26%
10 to 15 y.	12.5	8.92	2%	17.84%
15 to 20 y.	17.5	11.21	2%	22.42%
over 20 y.	22.5	13.01	2%	26.02%

(This makes it possible to highlight that in this example, the regulatory authorities use a 4.17% discount factor).

The commonly used method for determining the remaining net outstanding amount on each Gap_i interval and then to just refresh or update the loss or the increase in income due to an interest rate variation that this position provides identical results:

Formula 28

$$\pm 2\% . \sum_i \beta_i . Gap_i \leq 20\%. \text{ capital}$$

Basel III and banking leverage

Banks have access to the ECB for refinancing, thus transferring onto the central bank part of the counterparty risk. Even if it intervenes in the short-term with collaterals, haircuts and a senior position, it bears with governments a risk that the 2008 crisis, and even more the Greek and Cypriot crisis, made explicit. Banks, by the way that they are structured, are institutions that are used for leverage both in terms of capital and liquidity. The purpose of the solvency ratio is to limit this leverage. Introduced in 2007[46] and then adjusted in 2009, 2010 and 2011, the regulations issued by the Basel Committee are not fully settled. Ironically, the introduction of Basel II is most likely one of the technical cause that contributed to the amplification of the 2008 banking crisis. Exceptions that bankers successfully negotiated during the transition from Basel I to Basel II, in particular those pertaining to equity and on dividing net equity securitisation between tier 1 capital and tiers 2 capital, as well as the overconfidence given to rating agencies, created loopholes in regulations which investment banks used to create AAA bonds that actually did not meet the requirements of such a high rating.

The Basel Committee has perhaps not fully understood the lesson as it seems oblivious to government bonds that liquidity ratios it prescribes will push banks to acquire. Yet the overall regulations issued since 2008 are of exceptional quality and are undoubtedly key documents to refer to in order to comply with regulations, but also and especially to support reflections by bank management. It is quite surprising that in most institutions, their analysis is entrusted to specialists with the sole purpose of adapting the internal systems of the bank (which is certainly already a lot) and of lobbying in order to gain greater flexibility.

These texts emphasise constantly that they impose only minimum, in truth they exhibit an impressive range of fundamental issues for ALM and risk management. They are currently the first documentary source with regards to ALM (broadly) on all key areas of the profession. In particular, Pillar II, which is very often overlooked as it is more qualitative, is essential for decisions on ALM strategy. What clearly comes across is that the regulator has not quite settled on the finer details of this pillar. The crisis faced by Western governments will require that there be future limits on banks' risk-taking behavior and it is likely that the Basel Committee will transpose

---

[46] We refer here to the Basel Banking Committee on Banking Supervision (2011), initially developed in 2006, modified in 2009, completed in 2010 and revised in 2011: *Basel III: A global regulatory framework for more resilient banks and banking systems.*

some of its recommandations into stricter regulations: for example, it highlights the responsibilities of financial and other management, their responsibility to consider "even the most unlikely" situations that could threaten their institution. There still is no license for bank executives and therefore no risk of license withdrawal in case of rescue of the institution whose management is held responsible.

The Basel documents are extremely dense and rich. The committee, increasingly extends its reflections to the accounting banking norms. Additionally, we must not only look at Basel regulations as regulatory requirements but we must look at them as the spirit in which financial and risk executives must manage their institution. Hence the LCR is a minimum: it defines a crisis scenario and requires the institution to hold up to one month under certain hypotheses. The NSFR provides a customer asset objective / resource for a year. Bankers must ask the question of the evolution of these ratios over each period and anticipate their future value and hence provide the LCR on all subsequent years, to imagine other scenarios, other terms and to test its balance sheet.

Recalling Basel regulations

Basel II and its modified version, Basel III, define the level of capital to be held when faced with credit and market risk (as well as operational risk). Il There are many books explaining regulations, some of the most complex in the world, in their most subtle detail. In this matter, one must constantly refer to the Basel text and to the instructions of regulatory authorities.

Basel II introduced fundamental improvements in the risk management of a bank and in the capital estimation to protect from those risks. The three most significant changes are :

- The introduction of the method through an internal model,
- The improvement of various credit risk categories as well as the treatment of exposures related to securitization (the latter having been the subject to an addition within Basel III following the subprime crisis),
- A series of instructions and recommendations on banking supervision and market discipline.

Beyond technical changes in calculating capital requirements and thus in the optimisation of the consumption of capital and in the profitability of financial institutions, Basel II represents a revolution for bank branches since (1) regulatory measures are truly international and (2) it requires greater transparency, risk control and accountability on the part of the management team (Pillars II and III).

Although Basel II is logically promoting internal models that are more precise and rigorous, regulations still leaves banks the opportunity to use a so-called standard approach, when necessary or when the weakness of activity does not justify the investment in more complicated models.

Regulatory ratios

Capital requirements are the sum of:
- Capital requirements related to credit risk,
- Capital requirements related to market and counterparty risk,
- Capital requirements related to operational risks.

Market risk is treated as part of the CAD, it was improved under Basel III in light of the experience gained during the 2009 crisis (counterparty risk, lack of liquidity, credit derivatives, model risk...).

Operational risk translates into capital requirements based on a purely insurance-related statistical analysis, a type of analysis which is beyond the scope of finance. As this is an entirely separate issue, it lies outside the scope of this book. It will only be briefly mentioned[47].

Recall the three minimum ratios as defined in Basel III[48]:
- Core equity capital ratio (capital, issue premiums, income in reserve, disclosed reserves and OCI, minority holdings exhibiting the same characteristics): 4.5%
- Tier-1 ratio: 6%
- Overall Solvency ratio: 8%.

Banks are asked to create a capital "buffer" of 2.5% in core capital funds in normal times so as to comply during a period of crisis to these minimal

---

[47] It is nevertheless interesting to highlight the fact that every year, internal fraud amounts to several hundred events and external fraud amounts to hundreds of thousands of events. It is therefore a matter of great importance for the industry and for government, in particular with the development of internet.

[48] BCBS 189 page 12 "definition of capital" Provide more info on whether it is BCBS 2011 or 2013 that you are referring to.

regulatory requirements. If the bank is not able to build this "buffer", it undergoes a number of measures designed to force it to replenish its capital priority. In particular, its dividend payout ratio should decrease in proportion to the need for buffer reconstruction[49].

At last Basel III introduces a second countercyclical buffer to curb excessive credit growth, which is one of the causes and often a precursor of banking crises. Entrusted to each national regulator and based on a quantitative indicator methodology, the buffer could reach 2.5%. Banks will then incorporate, in direct proportion to their exposure of the given market, the additional need in capital requirement under the penalty of being restricted in their profit distribution in the same way as the "capital conservation buffer" of the previous paragraph[50]. Local regulators can already impose higher requirements when they seem justified: new activities, new shareholders, smaller banks ... If we look a little back with the new regulatory requirements, they remain reasonable and for most banks, they amount to endorsing their current situations: the requirement for minimum tier-1 core capital to 2.66% that we had previously were clearly insufficient in an economic environment that is as volatile as our current environment.

Capital accumulation

The regulation has evolved with Basel III by restricting all qualifying tier-1 items and by significantly increasing capital requirements. Furthermore, regulations have removed some of the flaws that still exist in the system:

- To get eligible for core capital, the non-voting stocks must have in particular characteristics that are identical to common shares, the bank should not be required to repay any of them, and the dividend can not benefit from any priority and should have a right to the net assets. Flexibility is however given to local regulators regarding cooperative banks.
- Tier-1 is reinforced and excludes super-subordinated debt with step up. Equity capital must meet 14 criteria. Nowadays to be eligible, in addition to common stocks and reserves, equity capital must be conditional, without guarantee, perpetual, with no

---

[49] According to a scale set by the regulator: under 5.125% of core tier-1, the bank must keep 100% of its income; 80% must be under 5.75%; 60% under 6.375% and 40% below 7%.
[50] With the same scale ratios: 100% conservation in the first quartile, 80% in the second, 60% in the third and 40% in the fourth.

incentive to be repaid and its dividend / coupon must be entirely discretionary, payable on the profits available for distribution and it must be non-cumulative (it can be chosen over regular dividend). It may be redeemable (callable) by the bank after five years with the authorisation from the regulatory authorities. Lastly, it should absorb losses from the non-payment of the coupon and either reduce its principal or ensure its automatic conversion into equity. We therefore obtain the following types of instruments :

- o super-subordinated perpetual non-cumulative bond callable after 5 years with absorbing mechanism via a nominal loss reduction or an automatic conversion into common equity shares under certain conditions of losses or of reductions of the solvency ratio.
- o Preference shares (which are not from common equity given that their dividend has priority and therefore does not meet criteria number 7 to be considered common shares).

- Tier-3 disappears.
- The OCI reserves are logically included (they are therefore deduced if negative) in tier-1, as long as they are considered as unrealized gains or losses. Cash flow hedge of item value in accrual (in L & R) are logically excluded, corresponding to many micro-hedging transactions on identified loan portfolios.
- Surplus capital in the fully consolidated banking and insurance subsidiaries attributable to the reporting entity, excluding minority interest, can be included, which means that the rest is no longer included. There is thus a full deduction of the CET1 capital funds of insurance subsidiaries [51] with one exception below the threshold of 10% of the bank's core capita. It is also worth noting

---

[51] Basel III regulations is a bit convoluted on the deduction of insurance companies' capital. Under Basel II, these were deduced at 50% from tier-1 and 50% from tier-2. Basel III regulations, section paragraph 84, asks for the reduction of tier-1 for capital amounts by the reporting entity beyond 10% of the "tier-1 common equity": this means that we can include them up up to 10% of the "common equity tier-1", with an overall 15% cap on the sum of the amounts that can be included. It is clear that this convoluted exception lacks real rational justification, but is probably issued from a compromise with the profession. In real life, while we can understand that the insurance sector regulator accepts a lower solvency ratio for the subsidiary of a large banking group - including rescuing it in case of problems -, the opposite cannot occur except during the sale of the entity (the increase in capital of the subsidiary to support the troubled bank is impossible except for capital surpluses beyond the safety margin required by the regulator).

that this deduction measure is simple common sense to the extent that the insurance sector regulator will never let a bank redirect capital from its insurance subsidiary should it be to the detriment of policyholders. The banks had also a competitive advantage over purely insurance groups, to the extent that they could re-use part of the capital of their own insurance subsidiaries to cover their banking credit risk (even if local regulators were to limit that possibility, as done in France with specific regulations regarding financial conglomerates).

- Goodwills and intangibles net from their DTL, the DTA net from DTL (which could therefore never be used) are deduced from CET1.
- Liabilities related to pension funds are to be deduced from CET1.
- Investments crossed with another financial institution (bank or insurance) must be deducted.

Credit risk

Two methods are used to calculate the weight of each asset (RWA) :

- The standard approach, which is providing weights based on external ratings. This method is close to the methodology applied under Basel I and is intended for small-scale entities and highly capitalized (or intended for marginal activities).
- The method based on an internal rating (IRB) that decomposes itself into two methods: a simplified methodology "the foundation approach" and a comprehensive methodology "the advanced approach". Major banks will need to use this method.

Standard approach

Banks must make use of external rating assessments. In case of multiple assessments, banks must use the worst of the two best assessments. The following table may be amended by local regulators.

Table 26

Credit assessment	AAA to AA-	A+ to A-	BBB+ to BBB-	BB+ to BB-	B+ to B-	Below B-	unrated
Sovereigns, central banks and assimilated PSE	0%	20%	50%	100%	100%	150%	100%
Public Sector Entities, banks, financial institutions Short Term (less than 3 month original maturity)	20%*	50% 20% ST	50% 20% ST	100% 50% ST	100% 50% ST	150%	50% 20% ST
Covered bonds (EEC)	10%	20%	20%	50%	50%	100%	20%
corporates	20%	50%	100%	100%	150%	150%	100%
Securitisation tranches (LT)	20%	50%	100%	350%	Deduction or 1250%		
Resecuritisation Exposures	40%	100%	225%	650%	Deduction or 1250%		
Retail loans, leases, credits…	75%						
Retail mortgages	35%						
secured commercial real estate	100% (or 50% under certain conditions at regulator's discretion)						
Securities	100% (out of other banks holding)						
Past due loans (over 90 days)	150% if prov < 20%, if not 100%						

* 0% for best multilateral development banks : World Bank, EIB…

Off-balance sheet items require a credit conversion factor "Credit Conversion Factor" (CCF) :

- CCF = 0% for commitments that are cancellable at any time,
- CCF = 20% for initial maturities of less than a year and 50% thereafter,
- CCF = 100% for the REPO, lending / borrowing securities (after taking into account collateral) …
- OTC derivatives additionally require an assessment of net exposure to risk :
    - For debt instruments: delta x notional x modified duration
    - For other: delta x notional value

Following the deduction of the collateral, the CCF is as follows:

Table 27

	CCF
Debt instrument of high specific risk	0.6%
Debt instrument of low specific risk that underlies CDS	0.3%
Exchange rates	2.5%
Gold	5%
Equity	7%
Other precious metals	8.5%
Electric power	4%
Other commodities	10%

The use of collateral requires to take haircut. Netting is also allowed.

The Internal Ratings Based approach (IRB)

The method uses internal estimates for:

- The probability of default (PD)
- Loss given default (LGD)
- Exposures at default (EAD)
- Effective maturity (M)
- The estimate of expected loss (EL) and unexpected loss (UL))

The weighting function provides the capital amount required to cover unexpected losses (UL), whereas the expected losses (EL) are to be covered by reserves.

Exposures are organized per category:
   a. Corporate exposure.

In addition to traditional lending, the regulator identifies 5 specialized subcategories 'specialized lending' (SL):

- project finance (PF),
- object finance (OF),
- commodities finance (CF),
- income producing real-estate (IPRE),
- high volatility commercial real estate (commercial real-estate) (HVCRE).

SMEs (with a turnover of less than € 50 mn) allow for weight adjustment depending on the size of the company.

   b. Sovereigns (include PSE and some MDBs)
   c. Banks
   d. Retail includes standard loans, mortgages, professionals and small and medium-sized enterprises (SME). The category is

divided into three sections: secured mortgages, revolving exposures in the retail portfolio, and the remaining.
  e. Equity (includes super-subordinated, convertibles and structured with a share equity component).

Two approaches are allowed:

- The "foundation" approach, wherein banks provide their own PD and use the settings of the supervisor to the rest (except for retail),
- The "advanced" approach in which banks use only their own parameter estimates.

The implementation of these methodologies is gradual for banks that have to build-up their historical data. We however already see the ranger of excessive confidence in figures and models, with teams becoming increasingly quantitative, to the detriment of qualitative analysis, which remains a fundamental part of assessment. But some elements vary structurally as has been shown in a number of examples in recent years:

- Thus the quality of subprime mortgages has deteriorated in the US in the 2006 vintages and especially the 2007 ones due to the easing of credit standards,
- In 2010, consumer credit loans in Italy saw their average amount double compared to 5 years before in some entities to order to bust revenues. Obviously, this policy increased CDL and LGD since it disregarded the customers' repayment capacity. The rationale was for lenders to increase their outstanding loans to those customers that appear to be good payers. Yet the customers' ability to repay based on income has slightly declined during the crisis and LGDs have shot through the roof with difficult litigations since many of the defaulted customers, previously perfectly solvent, fell victims of the aggressive marketing compaign of the bank...

Some markets are long-cycle markets. It will take years to establish a track record that will still need to be adapted to economic changes based on quantitative assessments.

Corporate, sovereigns or bank credits (specialized lending)

The calculation is based on a complex formula[52] derived from the 1987 Vazicek model for a homogeneous pool of risks that is characterized by infinite granularity:

- PD (Probability of Default) with a one-year time horizon (at minimum 0.03% for corporates and banks).
- LGD (Loss Given Default) is equal to 45% for senior loans and 75% for subordinated loans with the " foundation approach" and defined by institutions that use the "advanced approach".
- The collateral reduces the LGD after taking a haircut into account.

---

[52] Moulin (2012). We provide programming in VB:
Function Basel2_weight(PD, LGD, EAD, M) As Double
Dim Correlation, Maturity_adjt, capital_requirement As Double
M = Application.WorksheetFunction.Min(M, 5)
If PD = 0 Then Basel2_weight = 0 Else
  *Correlation = 0.12 * (1 - Exp(-50 * PD)) / (1 - Exp(-50)) + 0.24 * (1 - (1 - Exp(-50 * PD)) / (1 - Exp(-50)))*
  *Maturity_adjt = (0.11852 - 0.05478 * Application.WorksheetFunction.Ln(PD)) ^ 2*
  *capital_requirement = (LGD * Application.WorksheetFunction.NormSDist((1 - Correlation) ^ (-0.5) * Application.WorksheetFunction.NormSInv(PD) + (Correlation / (1 - Correlation)) ^ 0.5 * Application.WorksheetFunction.NormSInv(0.999)) - PD * LGD) * (1 - 1.5 * Maturity_adjt) ^ (-1) * (1 + (M - 2.5) * Maturity_adjt)*
  *Basel2_weight = capital_requirement * 12.5 * EAD*
End If
End Function

Table 28: Sample weights for an unsecured corporate/bank credit (rating agency's PD assessment, LGD = 45%) given the remaining maturity

Rating \ year	PD 1y	LGD	1	2	3	4	5
AAA	0.00%	45%	7.58	12.16	16.73	21.31	25.88
AA+	0.00%	45%	7.58	12.16	16.73	21.31	25.88
AA	0.01%	45%	7.58	12.16	16.73	21.31	25.88
AA-	0.01%	45%	7.58	12.16	16.73	21.31	25.88
A+	0.03%	45%	7.58	12.16	16.73	21.31	25.88
A	0.03%	45%	7.58	12.16	16.73	21.31	25.88
A-	0.05%	45%	11.22	16.84	22.46	28.08	33.71
BBB+	0.06%	45%	12.86	18.90	24.94	30.98	37.02
BBB	0.18%	45%	28.01	36.96	45.90	54.85	63.80
BBB-	0.49%	45%	51.59	63.18	74.77	86.36	97.94
BB+	1.06%	45%	75.14	87.88	100.61	113.35	126.08
BB	1.46%	45%	85.47	98.30	111.14	123.97	136.80
BB-	2.80%	45%	107.33	119.78	132.24	144.69	157.15
B+	4.15%	45%	123.00	135.11	147.21	159.32	171.42
B	5.71%	45%	139.00	150.89	162.78	174.67	186.56
B-	10.55%	45%	179.66	191.17	202.67	214.18	225.68
CCC+	15.93%	45%	209.17	219.99	230.82	241.65	252.47
CCC	17.83%	45%	216.38	226.91	237.44	247.97	258.50

Note: in the formula, the lower default probabilities are forced to 0.03% for banking and corporate loan.

Basel II provides a specific formula to address guarantees that are granted based on the probability of default of each entity and a correlation formula set by the regulator.

Specialized lending

For specialized credit activities, banks can use the IRB approach or use the following weights with the "standard approach":

Table 29

Sub-class	Strong	Good	Satisfactory	Weak	Default
Suggested rating	BBB- and better	BB+ or BB	BB- to B+	B to C-	D
PF, OF, CF, IPRE	70% (up to 50%)	90% (up to 70%)	115%	250%	0%
HVCRE	95% (70%)	120% (95%)	140%	250%	0%

(..) weight authorized based on validation by supervisors

PF: project finance; OF: Object Finance; CF: Commodities finance; IPRE: Income Producing real-estate; HVCR: high real-estate trading volatility.

Retail loans

Weights for retail loans are calculated based on three different functions, one for residential real estate, one for revolving loans and another for the rest. In each case, the default probabilities should be estimated directly by banks.

Table 30: Example of retail RWA

	Residential mortgages			revolving	other
PD	0.1%	0.2%	0.5%	3%	1%
LGD	25%	25%	25%	60%	45%
EAD	1	1	1	1	1
Weight	6%	10%	19.5%	51.5%	46%

Equity exposures

In the trading book, equity exposures in equities are treated as part of the CAD market risk. Outside the trading book, two approaches are possible:

- Market-based approach:
    - standard weighting method: 300% if the security is traded on an organized market (RSE), 400% otherwise. Netting is permitted.
    - Internal models: the capital charge is equal to the quarterly loss beyond the risk-free rate with a probability of occurrence of 1%. Nevertheless, the weight obtained cannot be less than 200% in the case of a security sold on a public market and 300% otherwise.
- The PD / LGD approach: PD is the internal estimate for 1.5 times the debt or corporate RWA (with M equal to 5 and LGD to 90%). Anyway, a minimum weight of 100% applies to long-term investments and to private equity (this encourages the financing of start-ups). For other types of investments, weights obtained may not be less than 200% in the case of a security traded on a public market and 300% otherwise.

Covered Bonds

Using the standard method, covered bonds meeting the definition of the European Directive on UCITS are weighted at 10% or 20% (UK, Italy, Portugal, Sweden, France, Belgium, Germany ...).

With the internal model, the vast majority of covered bonds receive particularly low weight: 4% with the "foundation approach" (LGD = 12.5% and M = 2.5 in CRD) and below in "advanced approach".

Securitization

Basel II was intended to better align capital weight with underlying economic risk, given the massive arbitrage that was allowed by Basel 1[53]. Regulations met this objective by making weights proportional to the PD and LGD and by applying stricter rules specific to junior securitization tranches. Basel III has strengthened the rules on conduits and re-securitizations which in fact no longer show interest for the banks because of their double weight compared to simple securitizations [54]. Basel II regulations were primarily based on rating agencies' independent risk assessment without actually considering the systemic impact of a massive model error on the part of the three major agencies, which is a technical cause of the subprime crisis. Basel III seeks to rectify that mistake by bringing forward the internal models and by treating re-securitisations (ABS CDOs) more harshly. Basel III introduces a safety margin for model errors. The structural risk of error remains but regulation reducing bank leverage, it is reduced. To this, a stricter outlook by regulators regarding complex market activities and regarding banks that have unconventional commercial activities. To weight their assets resulting from securitization, banks can choose again between the standard approach and the internal

---

[53] Under Basel I, corporates were all weighted at 100% and mortgages at 50% regardless of the true economic risk. Also banks were encouraged to leave their balance sheets good risks and structuring securitization transactions keeping the equity tranche, thereby concentrating the return and risk in order to increase their ROE. National regulators reacted by defining regulations but in a very international world, those regulations were easily circumvented.

[54] However, the regulator has not anticipated the usual infinite tranching ('mise en abîme') and the cubic-CDOs allow once again to circumvent the regulation .... However this limits arbitrage.

model approach. Capital requirements always depend on the existence of independent rating, or lack thereof.

- The banks must use the IRB approach based on external rating if it is available[55]. Consequently, weight will be inversely proportional to rating levels.

Table 31 :

securitisation	Senior tranche weighting
AAA	7%
AA	8%
A+	10%
A	12%
A-	20%
BBB+	35%
BBB	60%
BBB-	100%
BB+	250%
BB	425%
BB-	650%
Below and unrated	Deduction

- For securitizations having no external rating, IRB banks must use the "supervisory formula" which allows for capital consumption to be assessed depending on structural characteristics and exposure to the underlying asset.[56] The main parameters are the IRB consumption of the underlying pool of loans, the level of subordination and the thickness of the tranche and the granularity of the pool. Banks must apply each method according to the presence or absence of rating in instances where securitization contains both tranches that benefit from external rating and tranches without such rating.

Banks using the standardized approach must apply weights provided by the table above. In general, the weights obtained are higher than those of the IRB method even if the progressivity is reduced, allowing some

---

[55] Paragraph 609.
[56] Paragraph 609. The approach that consists of allocating internal rating is only possible for exposures to Asset-Backed Commercial Paper Programs (ABCP). In terms of liquidity and credit enhancement, these exposures must meet the terms of the conditions outlined in paragraphs 619 and 620.

optimizations: thus, all the BBB + BBB- tranches are assigned a weight of 100%. However, all units without rating must be deducted from tier-1[57].

Securitization remains a useful solution for banks and an optimization opportunity for two reasons. On the one hand from a technical point of view, rating agencies take into account the correlation effects. This contrasts with the regulator's approach and is a source of optimization. On the other hand, from a more strategic point of view, selling the equity tranche on an internal securitization allows for the "rental" of capital funds for a given term without recourse to the market. This is a flexible and discreet solution for banks that are a little short on equity. Banks generally compare the cost of capital funds that they recover once they meet their target return on equity. In fact, the reasoning must allow for a margin of flexibility because the capital "recovered" has the advantage of simplicity, discretion and flexibility, which justifies a small risk premium.

Operational risks

Financial institutions must hold capital in order to cover the risk of unexpected losses due to internal problems: faulty procedures and systems, fraud, human error, legal risks ... Three approaches are possible:
1. The basic indicator approach: 15% of the average gross bank revenue for three years,
2. The standard approach: 12-15% of gross revenues according to business lines,
3. The advanced measurement approach: the calculation is based on an insurance-statistical model approved by the regulatory authorities.

Calculating profitability net of risk

By imposing some sort of proportionality between risk and capital need, Basel II has emphasized the importance of calculating the net profitability of a credit transaction or of a business line. However from an economic point of view for management, it matters for the control of commercial activity: it is a clear example today that the risk and especially the cost of liquidity on French local authorities was poorly valued before the crisis due to the massive unbalanced position of Dexia which caused market disequilibrium.

---

[57] Under Basel II, that deduction was made at 50% only on tier-1 and 50% on tier-2, allowing *de facto* the reduction of capital funds consumption. Basel III has closed this regulatory loophole by logically imposing the entire deduction from tier-1.

On the contrary it offers real opportunities in parison to direct sovereign risk.

Formally, the profitability of an operation depends on the following parameters:

- Customer Rate CR.
- Rate of resource IRC provided by the ALM on the anticipated amortization profile for the portion of the loan not funded by capital (the IRC is supposed to include regulatory reserve requirements and other liquidity costs), to which the cost of options is added.
- Consumption of core capital: CC = RW (risk weight) multiplied by the target core capital funds of the institution. We assume that funding is provided for from these allocated capital funds (it actually is not exactly the case).
- Annual average cost of risk: EL
- Commission costs and income related to the nominal activity in percentage: m.

We therefore have ROE = [CR − (1 − CC). IRC − EL + m] / CC.

Table 32: ROE example

market	residential mortgages	revolving	other retail	Pub. Ent. AA 5Y	5Y corporate	5Y BBB corporate
nominal	100%	100%	100%	100%	100%	100%
PD	0.1%	3.0%	1.0%	0.01%	0.03%	0.18%
LGD	25%	60%	45%	45%	45%	45%
RWA	6%	51.5%	46.0%	14.8%	25.9%	63.8%
EL per annum	0.025%	1.8%	0.5%	0.005%	0.014%	0.1%
Capital funds (10% target)	0.60%	5.15%	4.60%	1.48%	2.59%	6.38%
financing	99.40%	94.85%	95.40%	98.52%	97.41%	93.62%
customer rate	2.95%	8.00%	4.50%	3.10%	1.95%	2.60%
TCI	2.1%	1.5%	1.8%	1.7%	1.8%	1.8%
margin before fees	0.825%	4.700%	2.250%	1.446%	0.137%	0.719%
ROE	**138%**	**91%**	**49%**	**97%**	**5%**	**11%**
modified duration	7	1	5	5	5	5
swap rate	1.50%	0.50%	1.10%	1.10%	1.10%	1.10%
Funding* against swap	50% covered + 40 bp & 50% + 80 bp	+ 100 bp	+ 70 bp	50% covered + 40 bp & 50% + 70 bp	+ 70 bp	+ 70 bp

*) Figures taken in November 2013 for an A bank except for revolving BBB

This simple calculation may have, if accompanied by an analysis of the long-term market, a significant impact on trade policy, as market share gains are (too) often made thanks to aggressive prices. Yet according to the example above, there are often wide variations in profitability per market based on the appetite of other risk actors: insurance companies, pension and management funds.

Basel III and liquidity monitoring

Liquidity management regulations harmonization at a global level is one of the great contributions of Basel III.

- The basic text [58] of *Basel III: A global regulatory framework for more resilient banks and banking systems* provides the general strokes of the reform and includes elements pertaining to liquidity,
- Core principles are defined in a second text from September 2008, *Principles for Sound Liquidity Risk Monitoring and Supervision*[59].
- Finally, the short-term ratio has been addressed by a January 2013 text: *Basel III: The Liquidity Coverage Ratio and liquidity risk monitoring tools*[60].

Texts, characteristic of the Basel Committee, are very dense.

Liquidity monitoring requires good modeling of future issuances by ensuring that they will be regular. In the different scenarios modeled, they will not generate an excessive degradation of cash reserves, which consists of the last adjustment variable.

In a structural fund income-generating bank capital, dynamic modeling should also include the expected future investments by category LCR (L1, L2a or L2b). The set therefore allows to calculate prospective LCR.

---

[58] reviewed in June 2011, see Basel Committee on Banking Supervision (2011)
[59] Basel Committee on Banking Supervision. (2008)
[60] Basel Committee on Banking Supervision. (2013)

Screenshot 16: Modeling anticipated LCR

Net Income		127,620.25	112,564.52	113,974.17	116,664.78
Dividends		11,860.94	11,331.51	11,358.19	11,554.13
ROE		9.03 %	7.35 %	6.89 %	6.55 %
Cost/Income Ratio		41.72 %	44.62 %	44.40 %	44.06 %
Periodic ROA		1.08 %	0.95 %	0.96 %	0.97 %
Yield - Actif		2.88	2.76	2.93	3.19
Yield - Liabilities & Equit...		1.4	1.51	1.72	2.02
RWA	4,878,097.4	4,955,672.43	5,097,285.42	5,128,051.05	5,100,214.72
Core Equity	912,665	1,021,224.3	1,115,257.32	1,210,673.3	1,308,583.95
Tiers 1	912,665	1,021,224.3	1,115,257.32	1,210,673.3	1,308,583.95
Regulatory Capital	922,665	1,031,224.3	1,125,257.32	1,220,673.3	1,318,583.95
Solvency Ratio on Core E...	18.71 %	20.61 %	21.88 %	23.61 %	25.66 %
Solvency Ratio Tiers 1	18.71 %	20.61 %	21.88 %	23.61 %	25.66 %
Solvency Ratio	18.91 %	20.81 %	22.08 %	23.80 %	25.85 %
Liquid assets	266,666.67	268,500	268,500	268,500	268,500
L1 Liquid assets	160,000	170,000	190,000	190,000	230,000
L2 Liquid assets	108,500	98,500	78,500	78,500	38,500
L2A Liquid assets	108,500	98,500	78,500	78,500	38,500
L2B Liquid assets					
Net Cash Outflows	121,103.58	82,997.76	89,330.99	76,670.67	75,759.45
Cash Outflows	301,103.58	331,991.04	357,323.97	306,682.67	303,037.8
Cash Inflows	180,000	297,123.09	404,347.51	522,422.91	658,245.76
Liquidity Coverage Ratio	2.2	3.24	3.01	3.5	3.54

Modeling the LCR is not a major issue provided that core balance sheet items are properly and globally entered. Moreover, the ratio experiences relatively slow changes on its customer items or other easily assessable items (cash flows and incoming and outgoing eligible investment lines). The ratio of the recovery measures are relatively simple and quick to implement: the establishment of a one-month notice for deposit redemption, the acquisition of eligible securities, reducing lines on financial counterparties...

Global liquidity analysis requires a considerable amount of time to assess the many effects. This is purely an analysis of modeling results given that indicators in this area do not project the overall effects that accurately. It is worth then noting that LCR methodology - which in fact defines a single scenario over a 1 month period - can readily be used to define other stress-tests by changing the parameters (deposit leakage percentage) and by summing up inputs and outputs over different terms.

The exercise requires discipline and careful attention to off-balance items: between funding commitments and margin calls on derivatives portfolios, there may be violent and delicate effects as they are crossed. The best example is constituted by the asset-swap portfolios of inflation of complex structures (snow balls ...) who can see their MtM literally explode during a crisis with a combination of several factors: falling interest rates, negative real interest rates, rising forward inflation expectations, the crashing of the yield curves...

Regulatory ratios and indicators

ALM uses a number of indicators. However all require a relevant banking modelization, in order to estimate their expected evolution. We sought here to group the main encountered indicators according to some key umbrella characteristics :

Market indicators

- CDS: this one is the most accurate market snapshot indicator on the institution's probability of default, as perceived by the market. Rating agencies use it to estimate the distance to default and to calculate PD (probability of default).
- Beta: the indicator can both be used for the entire banking sector or for a given institution.
- Spread between interbank and government rates.
- Lastly, given that banks are a reflection of the real economy, the state of the sector is generally correlated with the state debt spread, exchange rates volatility and corporate spreads.
- All these indicators nevertheless present the traditional weakness of market indicators: liquidity risk and herding phenomena.

Solvency indicators

- Solvency ratios CET1, T1 and RSE
- Capital / total assets
- RWA / Total Assets
- ROE and ROA

Credit Risk Indicators

- NPL / Total Loans

- Reserves / NPL[61]
- Cost of risk / loans NIM

Liquidity indicators

- HQLA / Assets
- Liquid assets / Assets
- Liquid assets / short term liabilities
- Customer assets / customer deposits
- LCR
- Short-term liabilities / total liabilities
- Short-term market liabilities / total liabilities
- Market liabilities / total liabilities
- Customers liabilities + equity / Liabilities
- NSFR
- Loans / assets

---

[61] The crossed reserves / total loans ratio is calculated at times, but it is dangerous because it does not differentiate between a low-risk and adequately provisioned bank and a high-risk and poorly-provisioned bank.

BALANCE SHEET MANAGEMENT

Funding policies

Available market tools

Apart from deposits, banks turn to the market for refunding. One of the fundamental questions of financial departments is then the choice of refunding tools and the amount allocated to each instrument.

- Short-term investment programs (certificates of deposit, CP, euro-commercial paper ...) and interbank market holds nowadays a prominent place in search for higher intermediation margin, but at the cost of greater liquidity risk. This is a simple structural method for a bank to refund itself. It is a matter of equilibrium between this short-term adjustment instrument and the structural needs of the institution.

- Long-term senior debt is the first and foremost a means to funding. In recent years it seemed less prominent. It nevertheless remains the most flexible, given that it is not tied to any asset. Issuances are limited by market absorption capacity and banks' concern not to pay too much for their refunding. It is worth noting that the gradual use by banks of refunding tools lowering the quantity of remaining available collateral in front of senior debt mechanically increases the cost of this senior debt.

- The use of covered bonds is expanding fast as countries adopt laws to legally secure the transfer of the collateral in case of default. They are governed at the European level by the 1988 UCITS Directive. Differing legal structures in different countries, some allowing all banks to issue covered bonds (Spain, Italy, Holland ...), while others require a specific license to issue covered bonds (Germany, Sweden, Portugal ...), whereas others require an SPE (France, Denmark, Ireland, Luxembourg ...).

    - The German Pfandbriefe market remains the predominant market in terms of size (greater than EUR 500 bn), liquidity and robustness. The use of the Pfandbriefe market is nevertheless limited by strict rules that govern it not only in terms of assets, but also in terms of valuation and over-collateralisation methods. Mortgages, aircraft and boats financing loans are all eligible as collateral. These three categories limit the refunding of debt up to 60% of a (conservative) collateral's assessed long-term value. Finally loans to local authorities constitute the fourth acceptable collateral (refunded at 100% of claims).

- The Luxembourg mortgage bonds market is more flexible.
- The French market is steadily growing.
- Finally, some issuances were made on the basis of European regulations.

Most EU countries have already adopted regulations on covered bonds: Belgium, Denmark, Spain (cédulas), France, Germany, Latvia, Hungary, Poland, Austria, Italy, Holland, Portugal, Sweden ... this now allows for diversified portfolios (there are currently about 300 issuers).

The covered bonds market nowadays is emerging as a robust and deep market (greater than EUR 2.8 trillion) - **it's the only one that was maintained during the crisis** even if spreads went from flat or negative (-4/5 bp) against E3M to+100/130 to bp - and is of low cost for the issuer. Its success lies in the fact that it also represents one of the only alternatives to Govies, with a very stable rating. Finally, ratings of covered bonds generally makes them eligible for ECB refunding (up to BBB-).

As for all collateralised assets, the fact remains that it is necessary to analyze the structure and quality of issuers of a collateral: a covered bond on German and French real estate mortgages does not present the same risk than a covered bond on shipping or aircrafts, or a cédulas multi-issuer. Regulators have certainly committed to ensure the professionalism and the soundness of the collateral issuing entities' management. However the main risk is related to the underlying asset: the cédulas market had robust control, yet it was logically affected given that the housing bubble burst. In a market where property values dip over 30% of their initial value, covered bonds' ratings will irreversibly suffer. And if issuing banks are not bailed out, assets may be directly affected.

In case of default, the issuer loses control of the credit pool that is used as collateral for covered bonds. An administrator is appointed to manage assets, collects cash flows and pays back the various covered bonds holders, these being equal (there lies the main difference with the RMBS which are isolated by their pools; their management is from the start entirely separate from the originating bank or banks).

However covered bonds during their life cycle, are first and foremost a debt incurred by the bank, benefit from their rank of seniority in the scale of the debts of the latter. They additionally benefit from the overall bank incomes to service their debt and the quality of their collateral benefits from the substitution mechanism of doubtful or disputed debts. Finally, as bank debt, they do not entail strict adequacy between their duration and the duration of the underlying assets.

Covered bonds are now the most stable and cheapest long-term market funding tool. Credits are not taken out of bank balance sheets (even in France, where the specialised issuing firm benefits from a promise of debt only transfer), therefore their issuance has no effect on the bank's own capital funds consumption. However, they become part of overall liquidity ratios and are even generally by extension considered as customer deposits. Finally, they are eligible for LCR as tier 2A assets (15% haircut). Their large market, the duration of their issuances, which is superior to all other tools, the quality of their collaterals, the strict regulations around them and the required over-collateralization makes them actually essential to banks nowadays.

- ABS / RMBS: securitizations immediately remove the assets from the originators' balance sheet. From then on their management is separate from that of the original entities. If they are protected in the case of default of the original entities, however, they can only rely for the service of their debt on the quality of the assets initially transferred. Leaving credits out of the balance sheets, they allow for an immediate reduction in RWA. By allowing the tranching of debt between super-senior tranche, senior, mezzanine, equity, they optimize the refunding costs of the bank. Note that tranches above BBB- are also eligible for ECB even if the haircut is significant (26% in BBB). Securitization finally provides funding for loans that are non-eligible to covered bonds: it is therefore a complementary and specific tool.
- Direct sale of asset. A legal variant of securitization is the direct sale of loans. The market increases in size with the search for diversification of major institutions and hedge funds. Removing loans from your balance sheet may be due to a number of reasons: in case of decrease in interest rates, it often helps to externalize underlying profit if there is no micro-hedging swap to jointly break. This obviously removes risk and it reduces trivially balance sheet assets.

- Sale of assets with granting of a warrantee: the tool, less known, consists of selling a set of loans and providing a guarantee concurrently on the performance of the loan. Depending on the legal scheme, there is usually no significant economic transfer of risk and loans can remain in the balance sheet in terms of accounting (there is no deconsolidation). However, the fact of granting the guarantee allows the bank to benefit from cheaper indirect funding (even if it is generally more expensive than covered bonds due to illiquidity). This scheme therefore has characteristics that mirror covered bonds: the investor enjoys the guarantee from the start of the transferred assets while benefiting from the originator's credit.

- Technical differences: credits, REPOs and other collateralised issuances. The structures described above may be restructured in order to guarantee other legal forms of refunding. The simplest is the contraction of credit collateralized by the AAA tranche of a securitization retained by the bank. This tranche can also be placed in REPO (sale followed by a repurchase agreement). Both methods were used extensively during the crisis particularly for dollars-based refunding. Some private transactions have also been secured by receivables under private law contracts (commitment of transfer). The lender then takes a legal risk in exchange for a greater collateral and a quality that is satisfactory to it.

- ECB: the last source of funding for a bank is of course its ability to access ECB funding. This funding is systematically collateralised according to clear regulations. Apart from the LTRO (long-term refinancing operations, that was exceptionally set up by the ECB since the crisis), funding by the ECB remains short-term but to the extent that its renewal is very predictable, institutions can afford a certain liquidity risk. While central banks may refuse funding if they believe the institution is at risk, in fact, like during the Greek crisis, they maintained credit lines to institutions that were clinically dead, pending recapitalization. Central banks generally act more gently by ensuring the refunding but by requiring the establishment to reduce their assets or to recapitalize. The use of ECB lines of credit is therefore a sensitive tool: flexible and very inexpensive, banks have there an almost artificial means of inflating their NBI without commercial activity. But the role of ECB funding is not explicit and central banks remain vigilant that the use of credit lines remains confined to their primary role of lender of last resort and for short-term liquidity adjustment. The flexibility they tend to provide a little more currently in terms of amount and duration is clearly[62] linked to the fact that the mechanism helps banks to replenish their incomes while providing indirect funding to states (the simplest and most leveraged trade being the purchase of state debt and refunding it through the ECB)

What tool, for which purpose, and to what extent?

Once the funding program is defined in terms of duration and size, there remains the choice of instruments to implement the funding program. If the goal is to raise liquidity only, it makes sense to exclude direct securitizations. Even if they provide liquidity, they have as main function to transfer credit risk and / or to provide savings of capital (excluding structuring fees), for an additional cost.

In long-term funding, the main issue beyond the related operations mentioned above (REPOs on credit or ABS that are held internally ...) is to define the portion of covered bonds issued versus senior debt. Many covered bonds have the advantage of:

- price which improves the outcome and stability of the result, reducing the institution's PD,
- market depth, it also allows to investors to be familiarised with the signature.

But this runs the risk of:

- potentially consuming collateral reserves in case of a crisis,
- using the limits of the market on its covered bond own signature, reducing the possibility of a successful additional issuance in case of crisis,
- increasing the LGD of the institution because the senior creditors will not have access to the best assets,
- subsequently rolling over senior debt and weakening its liquidity.

There is no study known to the author that models the optimal amount of covered bonds to hold relative to senior debt. It is not clear that such modeling gives also significant results. Indeed, it is preferable first to carry out issuances as regularly and homogeneously as possible. Moreover, it is

---

[62] For eligible collateral, see European Central Bank (2015).

under this condition that covered bonds can be considered as customer deposits and not as market resources.

The second strategic issue is the use of securitization: is it a technique to be used opportunistically or is it better to have a regular risk selling policy? Most banks entrust these operations to their market teams, knowing that still too often banks do not like to sell their credits. Conversely, the practice of syndication is widespread and accepted. Yet securitization allows for great flexibility in the design of tranches and creating pools against syndication which amounts to the outright sale of credit. Thus, securitization enables the bank to capture a larger share of incomes generated by its business when its credit is introduced at market price. This is also a second argument for the routine use of this technique: the securitization confronting the bank to institutions other than its local peers enables it to benchmark its credit price against the market. The investors' universe is of course different from that of the covered bonds. These investors are highly specialized, pushing their studies before decision-making, more demanding and more international, they adjust their prices in times of crisis and must then often reduce their investment because of withdrawals from their customers. Nevertheless, they constitute a growing segment of investors and it is unfortunate that most banks do not use them.

Securitization allows for fine and discreet management of its risks. The banks have an incentive to always keep this operational option, and even to adjust the size of their issuances rather than their pace of issuance.

Steering through customer business

Steering a bank in the long-term is done through business activity. Financial strategies and especially hedging strategies are used only to buy time in order to adapt production facilities to the new environment, as we have seen. Accordingly, the first balance sheet management tool is customer business. Even if the measures are slow to implement, once implemented they are permanent. Financial departments have therefore a fundamental role in steering business activity both in terms of credit structuring and in terms of deposits.

In terms of credit, even if rate structures can be controlled relatively easily, durations are strongly linked to customer needs and thus to the customer segments. The choice of these segments is essential to maintain a balanced position. The most famous example of imbalance remains Dexia with an extremely long duration asset that no other segment rebalanced enough (nor any long-term liabilities).

On deposit collection, the difficulty lies in its stabilization. Customers always wish to have liquidity clauses when needed, which is natural, given that we observe that they do not overuse such clauses (excluding institutional rational pricing) and on the contrary, they appreciate being supported in the build-up of precautionary savings. Therefore, the key to savings stability remains the legal and commercial clauses beyond interest rate: one month's notice for the LCR, regular debit instruction on the current account to provide savings, loyalty bonuses ...

Managing capital surplus

The management of an institution's capital funds surplus stems from a few simple rules and from common sense:

- A bank's capital funds are the raw material that allows it to function. They must therefore be invested in a safe manner and especially must not risk being tapped into should there be a crisis.
- Capital funds are an important part of an institution's balance sheet. They should be invested so as to generate reasonable profitability.
- For the financial institution, capital funds are the longest term liability. They can be invested long-term.

Once these three basic rules are implemented, we get a gradual, long-term and diversified investment strategy:

- Gradual because the bank will be in a position to gradually increase its exposure as it has access to unrealized capital gains and a higher solvency ratio. Graduality also requires investment policy consistency and therefore a patient long-term investor attitude and having well simulated risks for its investment and regular portfolio review.
- Long-term means that capital should not be invested in the short-term unless there is major risk to the institution which makes management give up on profitability in order to favor the liquidity of its assets. Indeed, on a normal interest rates curve, that is to say *in contengo*, the investment of capital must be able to capture the

differential between the short-term and long-term rates. The long-term also means that the credit line renewals must be gradual and balanced over time.

- Diversifying is a general investment rule. For a bank, diversification must take account of regulatory constraints and of its market segment (buying bonds from the companies that are its clients for loans or companies that are strongly linked to its clients is not a diversifying investment). Diversification means that a bank must invest in different possible asset classes: real estate, bonds, equities, alternatives ... But always through a cautious and rational approach.

The first asset class will obviously be bonds from non-financial institutions : state bonds, covered bonds, corporate bonds and Elligible Path Through with initial long durations (generally they are above five years). Credit risk will then follow a similar selection process to institutions' bank loans.

A stock portfolio, even if capital fund consuming, has a place in long-term allocation. However, it should be built up gradually, from securities on which visibility is good: a long history of positive cash flows, solid commercial positions ... This excludes most of the so-called growth stocks that should be part of a separate pocket, limited, due to its uncertainty. Gradual portfolio construction does not mean one should buy constantly. Stock market cycles are brutal and it is known that the PER can vary widely. A stock portfolio, to be sure, must be acquired on reasonable ratios.

The construction and modeling of a balanced investment portfolio is a classic topic [63]. It determines the probabilities of loss on the portfolio. From then, the issue is to define the leverage that can be allowed on these investments linked to the investment of capital funds [64]. This topic intersects with constraints on the balance sheet total and maximum limits of acceptable loss for the institution. If it remains in its VAR limits, there is no foreseeable reason to prohibit leverage on investments. In fact it is often healthier than to

---

[63] See the extensive financial literature on CAPM and VAR calculations.
[64] Formally, the CAPM states that there is an optimal portfolio with "no risky asset" and that any portfolio made out of this optimal portfolio and of risk-free interest rate is optimal but with different ER and variance. The choice of leverage in this model is to define the part that is risk-free (here, short since there are loans) for the risk level sought by the institution.

incorporate the same leverage directly into some investments (where it is less controllable).

Related financial and commercial activities

Peripheral financial and commercial activities are a subject in itself. We define as such income generating activities other than the management of the long-term portfolio. Every bank holds this type of activity:
- Small arbitration desk
- Business promotion or property management
- Private equity structure ...

Often starting from a good idea and / or the specific capacity of a banking team, they may offer an opportunity with little risk. However, past observation of their incomes is often inconclusive: negligible incomes compared to the bank's size to excessive energy expenditure, operational risks that comes up when the decision to exit the business, bad appreciation of real risk of non-core activity ... Banks are still struggling to accept that some activities, out of core business, even if they would be able to profit from them, are just not part of their job and are a waste of time and energy while the customer service can always be improved. If from an ALM perspective, we always prefer simple features, experience shows that as soon as there is too much complexity in an institution, there is risk of damage to the heart of business and its equilibrium.

Bank bail-outs

The financial litterature does not discuss a lot the management of crisis situations. Yet failed banks are not new, and outside major transactions (savings & loans, Crédit Lyonnais, Lehman Brothers, Bear Stearns ...), many institutions disappear regularly (Barings, CPR ...) or are the subject of discrete bail outs (cooperative banks regularly experience situations of the sort). Since the 2008 crisis, this has renewed interest to the point that the regulator now requires writing by the institutions of the measures that they would consider in case of difficulty.

The bail-out of a facility is divided into a number of phases that are close to unavoidable.

Three phases of a bail-out

The first is to stop the bank's liquidity haemorrhage with infusion from either the central bank or a lifeguard called for support. Banks die liquidity loss, regardless of the underlying cause, as a man with lung cancer dies of asphyxiation as the lungs can no longer supply the body with oxygen necessary for life. This phase provides anywhere from a few hours to several days of respite. For investors, the infusion is often the signal of imminent death or of clinical death. ELA (the central banks' credit lines without any real guarantee) can be likened, in their role, to morphine pumps. At high doses, they are a sign of inevitable death, they relieve pain without treating the underlying cause which generally only gets worse. The Lehman Brothers collapse demonstrated that the uncoordinated failure of an institution can trigger devastating deflagration, beyond the absorption of existing losses in the institution's balance sheet. The question of whether to use an ELA infusion or the support of an intermediary cannot be decided ahead of time. However, the second option, although it is politically attractive for the state, often leads to the transfer of the cancer to the banking sector on a larger scale, as was the case in Spain (as the Spanish saying goes "by mixing a glass of mud with a liter of milk, one gets a liter of mud ...". The same issue was observed in the US with Wachovia. Such a solution is often imposed by the government (like in the Spanish example). It can also throw the target into the arms of a stronger player, regardless of the financial interests of the shareholders of the troubled bank (in the Bear Stearns case, the situation was even more dramatic as the employees were essentially paid in shares). For the community, through the state as its representative, to take guardianship of the institution does not necessarily mean nationalizing all losses in the first place, or the losses faced by shareholders. The authorities were actually caught off guard at the beginning of the crisis, they did not know the issue, they did not measure the extent of the problem and they were afraid of the reaction of shareholders, while the capitalist game is very clear that shareholders lose their investments in case of default.

The first phase also requires to the existence of a bail-out team that is ready to act in support of management or as a substitute to management if the latter is no longer psychologically able to remain in management.

These few hours of respite allow for an initial diagnosis in order to understand where the crisis stems from and where exactly in the balance sheet are the problematic assets (these can also be healthy assets that are poorly funded) so as to assess the potential real losses, their dates of occurrence and the cost of exiting toxic assets at market prices.

The diagnosis is key because it is out of the diagnosis that the way to stop the liquidity haemorrhage stems. There are two potential options:
1. To cut off the diseased part from the healthy part while seeking to stabilize the latter.
2. To smooth out over time the losses that will then be absorbed by future incomes vintage, even if this means recapitalizing the institution in order to strengthen its solvency.

In both cases, generally liquidity infusion should be maintained. In both cases, the communication on the will of any guarantor, and its capacity to maintain its position, is key. The credibility of the decision depends on its validation or lack thereof by the markets.

Between the two options, the selection depends on several parameters. The first is the extent of loss and where it occurs. Very high losses that have destroyed capital can usually be absorbed without suspicion and therefore without disruption to business activity. Fortis is a typical bail-out case with the separation of toxic assets from sound business activities. Dexia is a mixed example with a separation of the healthy commercial activity, namely the Belgian activity which benefits from deposit to refund the credit business, now in Belfius while the overall structure is only keeping the problematic positions. Indeed, they were of such size and so connected to the banking business model that the overall portfolio was placed in run-off. Most German banks are a prime example of recapitalization. For Commerzbank, it was a success because losses were reasonable in nature. For the Landesbanks, it was mainly a political choice (which ultimately was not viable). RBS is another example of bail-out by maintaining the entity, despite the huge losses (and therefore in spite of the rules mentioned above). The choice was political and probably linked to a poor assessment of the situation [65]. The recapitalization of French banks is an example where the

---

[65] It is very interesting to analyze the November 2013 decision of the British government to liquidate the bad bank by raising the following points:
- The size of the "bad bank" (currency 38 bn.) is relatively small compared to total assets (currency 846 bn.) but atrophied in terms of RWA (currency 116 bn.). RBS did not have a funding problem with its bad bank, but rather had consumption issues with regards to equity and unrealized losses estimated between currency 4 and 5 bn..
- The bank is state-owned at 80% which means that GBP 1 bn. of these losses are currently carried by private shareholders.
- The "good" bank suffers from insufficient profitability (with a C / I ratio which is too high) and flagging business development.

- RBS holds non-core assets including Citizens, its US subsidiary (currency 117 bn. of balance sheet total ti currency 18 bn. capital) who started to clean its accounts and ULSTER Bank which has not yet completed the exercise and which is a source of losses.

The decision to simply sell the "bad bank" over two years and to take the loss by financing it through the sale of Citizens Bank is explained by the fact that 20% of this loss will be borne by private investors and that, after 5 years of life "with its bad bank", the separation exercise would have involved a significant operational risk (there were a lot of complex contracts) whereas many risks were due to expire within two years.

It is more interesting to look at an analysis of the RBS situation after 5 years of life with a "bad bank":

- the bank has constantly tried to straddle the fence. Consequently, it sold insufficient amounts of its bad assets and to compensate for losses, it reduced its business activities and sold good assets: the mix of both generated a "lack of strategic coherence."
- management still wanted to keep the prestigious CIB activity. This diverted it from its accountability to the British economy and accounts for the poor commercial performance in its core British market business.
- management did not focus on the management of the commercial bank. Consequently, the C / I ratio is bad and therefore income generation is insufficient to absorb losses.
- the bad bank has consistently absorbed the profits of other business activities and in the end, it did not help in reviving the good bank that it had stifled.

Finally, it is interesting to understand the motivations underlying the decision of simply taking the loss by the bank rather than splitting RBS:

- 20% of loss is borne by the private investor.
- the government was afraid that the creation of a separate bad bank would be distracting to management: the argument is surprising because in fact, leaving the bad bank in their management actually distracted them.
- the creation of a bad bank was deemed to be complicated.
- government did not wish to provide currency 38 bn. funding: here again, the argument is surprising because RBS could have assumed the bulk of this super-senior funding and the structure could have set up a Government Guaranteed Commercial Paper (GGCP) program.

This report confirms a posteriori that the wrong decision was taken in 2008 when it was decided not to split RBS into a healthy small-sized institution concentrated state has simply provided short-term support to companies that were able to manage alone their difficulties both in terms of losses on assets and on market funding. The solution of preferential securities contribution[66] had the merit of signalling that the French state was ready and had the capacity to support its banks in order to reduce pressure on its banking sector.

The second parameter to consider in this fundamental strategic choice is that of the nature of the losses. Losses, even large, but that are clearly separate from sustainable commercial activities are more naturally separatable (the case of Fortis) that losses related to the collapse a core commercial banking business (the case of the Irish and Spanish banks) or of its business model (case Dexia). The latter is the most difficult to diagnose because it requires having an understanding of fundamental market changes. Dexia would have survived a cyclical closure of liquidity, but its business model was overly based on a massive liquidity transformation to withstand a revaluation of prices and of liquidity risk on a global scale. Another case where the separation was needed beyond any doubt is the case of Iceland: Iceland's economy was not able to take on the risks taken by its banks abroad and had indeed no reason to do so. Indeed, these institutions clearly benefited from the error of rating on the country in order to engage in operations that were totally separate from their economic functions for Iceland. Therefore, there was no reasons to ask the Icelandic taxpayer, already heavily affected by the massive currency devaluation, to assume the losses that had nothing to do with its economy. Only the shareholders and creditors had to accept the consequences. Conversely, the state had to support the Icelandic part of its major banks

---

on England and a bad bank in run-off with private shareholders totally discarded in favor of the state.

The current decision is also linked to the fact that the carrying of assets must not bring much more than their sale at present value at the cost of normalized capital . Most of the loss is indeed already in the accounts and included in the valuation. Finally, from a political point of view, a bad bank is always a sensitive issue for a government that avoids the problem through liquidation.

In the end, what the government announced is actually the restructuring of RBS and the absorbtion of most of the loss.

[66] The state had chosen this solution to minimize its risk and to receive regular income which partially offsets tax losses related to the fall in income. The alternative would have been to force banks to recapitalize by providing guarantee for the operation in exchange for a commission guarantee. Thus in the absence of private recapitalization, the state would become a shareholder at a more attractive price ...

despite their mismanagement of euro-based loans to customers whose incomes were in Icelandic krona.
The third parameter is to appreciate the disruptive nature of the losses in daily business management. But this aspect is often overlooked when in fact it is key. An area of loss is akin to a sword of Damocles hanging over the heads of management, it diverts attention from other needs of the bank and maintains a poor internal climate with repeated poor results as and when the entity absorbs losses related to past activities.

The second step is the bail-out itself: it amounts <u>to cutting out the diseased branch</u>, that is to say, to stop the activities that are affected in order to focus on the heart of business and to restore the institutions' solvency. Then there is a second decision to be made if the institution chooses to keep its balance sheet activity in liquidation: is it better to take the loss instantaneously, which is the US method or is it better to smooth it over time, which is usually the course of action in Europe? The choice still depends on the three conditions laid out above. The first requires to then also assess loss in market value, to calculate the impact on the capital, to estimate the hope of recovery and the income generation capacity of the institution during this phase. Generally, it is always better to take the loss as quickly as possible, that is if we can recapitalize. To maintain unrealized losses on a balance sheet is not only a sword of Damocles as mentioned above, but it also generates a fatigue phenomenon with teams whose efforts are drained in the absorption of past losses.

This operational step may be the work of the institution itself (the case of low losses that do not requiring massive recapitalization) or may require bail-out by a third party. This is the most delicate moment of bail-outs psychologically because many managements generally refuse to take their losses when they appear to be manageable or to be simply carried forward into the future (while hoping that the market improves). The choice is often too painful for many because it requires admitting mistakes.

In parallel to this cleaning of the accounts operation, the institution will need to be <u>recapitalised</u>. The key question is by whom and at what cost. When it comes to a private investor acting in a free and rational way, this question does not arise and this solution should be sought in the first place, even if it means that, as with Fortis, the state assumes certain risks (such as carrying a toxic position). It is obviously more difficult when it comes to a purely state-backed bail-out. During the crisis, the states have been surprisingly understanding and reluctant to sanction private investors. A rational attitude would rather be on the contrary that any recapitalization by the state would be either confiscatory in nature or massively dilutive for the current shareholders, so as to push them to seek first and foremost a private solution. If they cannot, since the bank went under its regulatory ratios or is in default, it is in fact in a state of bankruptcy. Government intervention should be seen that in order so as to avoid the domino effect of this bankruptcy and to protect the customer savings. Seen in this light, it seems legitimate that the private shareholder, bankrupt, is taken out of the institutions' capital. For the author, public authorities should be able to impose even more severe haircuts on institutional senior debts as well as on the interbank market. This perspective could probably only push institutions to merge and their creditors to maintain their funding in case of a liquidity crisis.

In the case of a joint bail-out where the state sells part of the institution, the latter must have great maneuvering capacity since it must act in a context of emergency and without the risk of legal obstacles being raised to block it (it is certain that the bankrupt shareholders will contest the bankruptcy of their business). Regulations are heading in this this direction by strengthening the regulator's power to seize and requiring that institutions draft their wills in case of default.

Defeasance structures

Defeasance structures or the ring-fencing of assets are intended to relieve the healthy part of the institution so that it can be easier to sell. Transfer of a portfolio to an SPV with its funding is done in two phases:

In the first phase, the establishment or holding structure remains the owner. So there is no consolidation impact. The advantage of this step is that through the transfer of assets and liabilities, it allows for bypassing issues linked to valuation. Asset transfer auditors (commissaires aux apports) should provide advice on its overall valuation. In general, assets have clearly a market value that is lower than their transfer value. However it is often the same with liabilities, which in market value can be valued as own debt, thus may undergo strong discount during a crisis. The transfer allows for the reevaluation of liabilities, which is not possible on the balance sheet itself. And finally, the asset transfer auditors value those by looking also at the overall equilibrium: assets valued above market but funded so that they remunerate capital funds without major ALM risk will provide an overall positive valuation of the net assets, which is the goal.

During the second stage, there must be significant economic transfer, so as to deconsolidate the structure. This necessarily requires an investor external to the entity to enter into the SPV capital. To let a state structure enter this entity, as observed regularly during the crisis, has two advantages: there is no accounting constraints on the acquisition value, a simple opinion of the asset transfer auditors is sufficient for the investment to be valued at its acquisition price. The difficulty lies in the fact that the structure must not be consolidated in public debt. Eurostat published a number of criteria to decide on whether or not to consolidate the structure [67]:

- Structure's independence of management and decision-making [68],
- Full risk transfer to the SPV so as to develop a financial intermediary. It should be noted that the ESA95 2.33 regulation requires risk-taking but not necessarily.
- Investment must comply with the capital injection test [69] and the government must show that it acts as a private investor. The easiest way for this is to co-invest with private investors and to prove that performance is acceptable. Note that this does not necessarily need to be a minority stake for the state.

If these criteria are met, there is no consolidation of the entity and the investment has no impact on net debt, since the asset is also valued at its acquisition value.

The great difficulty with this type of operation is often linked to liabilities because if the assets are complex, most of the time, they can't be fully refunded on a stand alone basis (even if management allows for restructuring, for opportunistic sales …). Thus most structures enjoy state guarantee for their debt issuance. In this case, guarantees must be given at market price to be accepted by Eurostat and by the European Commission.

The final step consists in receiving authorisation from the European Commission's Competition Directorate: a defeasance structure is to provide the business entity with assistance. If it is provided by the state, there is an unfair advantage in the economic game. The European Commission will then open a file to verify that this state intervention is warranted, relevant and reasonable. In particular, the Commission will verify that competition will not be distorted by the arrival of a new player benefiting from unfair advantage. Thus, a defeasance structure is but a tool at the disposal of a comprehensive state strategy: if it decides to intervene in support of an

---

[67] Eurostat (2014).
[68] Eurostat (2014), p. 32
[69] Eurostat (2014), p. 113.

institution, it is that the collapse of the latter would have had an unacceptable impact on society and that it was better to deal with the problem in the long-run. This means that to "take care of the problem", the state must define its ultimate goal: merging of the business entity to a foreigner in order to diversify its domestic market as well as to attract a financially powerful entity (the Fortis strategy), the fusion of the business entity with another local player to reduce competition (the Spanish strategy), the privatization of the business entity or its repositioning as a public sector service provider. Reading through the successive decisions of the European Commission shows that each of them was extremely reasonable and understanding with the states, the constraints that it included most often were in fact sound management commitments (no unfair competition under the aegis of the state) and exit strategies did not even have to be a firm commitment. Experience shows also that by working in harmony and transparency with the European Commission teams, we get far superior results when compared to results from a strategy of confrontation.

Guarantees

States like to provide guarantees that have have numerous advantages from their point of view:

- The state is only exposed to real losses since it is not concerned with the MtM, whereas by valuing the guarantee, the entity removes a part of the MtM,
- This has no immediate budgetary cost, as losses appear later and in a manner that is smoothed over time,
- This generates income on the guarantee premium.
- There is an alignment of interest between the entity and the state as soon as the bank is still exposed in first loss, for instance, and / or risk participation.

The rule on the first diagnosis stated previously applies here too. The main criteria for resorting to providing guarantee, rather than to resort to restructuring the core of the entity, is itself dictated by the magnitude of the losses. These must remain reasonable both in terms of balance sheet size than in the financial institution's capacity to absorb the underlying losses. Indeed, one must be cautious that the perspective of the institution for the next 10 years are not limited to the absorption of past losses, whether directly or through the payment of a guaranteed premium. Good examples of guarantees include the governmental support to bank issuances at the height of the crisis. In France for instance, financial institutions were sound and the state merely prevented them from being affected by market failure by providing guarantee for long-term issuances. All institutions have paid, no loss was observed and the market has gone back to normal. The intervention was therefore limited. Collateral and additional capital made available to KBC assets by Flanders and the Federal State are another example that is more complex. KBC has already started to pay off and it is clear that the bank has the ability to get out of that support by itself.

Collaterals thus appear as a good solution to short-terms rather than structural problems. ALM modeling of the institution after the implementation of support must show an outlook that is acceptable for the planned term and for exit after a few years term.

The banker's traps

This last part is different from previous ones since the author abandons the technique and methodology to get back to the fundamental value of a bank, namely, the people that make-up the bank. No model, no business plan will help ensure the success of an establishment better than relevant choices made by its managers and employees, starting with its management. This fact was "somewhat" forgotten before the crisis [70]. Yet it is the major issue for bank management and unfortunately no method, no regulation, can fully protect the company against the human risk to which institutions are exposed.

The capacity to face one's mistakes

The past few years have provided us with plenty of insights with regards to issues with the management of financial institutions. However here too, it is still necessary to take a break, to put down one's pencil, to forget the daily maelstrom of business, which is generally too slow, of customers who complain, of dissatisfied employees, to take a little step back to analyze the reasons for failures and for successes observed during the crisis. This seems obvious and yet the first glaring error of many institutions has been and still remains their inability to reflect on their past mistakes. These are buried, if possible attributed to previous management teams, repressed in a taboo area of the company's collective memory. They are certainly the topic of confidential one-on-one discussions but rarely does one observe a calm and thorough process where the steering committee faces reality. It is as if men were concerned that this type of exercise, which in the author's eyes is absolutely necessary, would run into into a process of settling scores or would damage their reputation or the one of their institution, which is typical of human psychology. Mao Tse-tung, before sinking into the monstrosity of public humiliations, won a revolution in the face of an army which was superior initially from a military point of view thanks to the quiet and reflective analysis he did with his staff of his army's mistakes. His writings on strategy emphasise strongly the usefulness of such an approach. It is true that his writings from the peak of his intellectual strength are now abandoned because of the crimes following his rise to power. Nevertheless, Mao merely applied Asian wisdom which is already visible in Sun Tzu. Many institutions would benefit from reflecting in a more fundamental manner about their failures. The author has repeatedly tried to encourage

---

[70] Personal testimonies are italicized to highlight a character different from the rest of the book. The author uses the first person for the same purpose of differentiation.

groups to have day long meeting behind closed doors with their steering committee to give thought to the structural reasons (organizational errors, misalignment of interests) and human (incompetence, short-term gain culture ...) of their failures. For many organizations, the exercise was still clearly too painful, which says a lot about the psychological maturity of a number of executives. They are focused on the system rather than on the result of reflection on human experience and professional competence.

Humility and moral courage

The psychological process is an interesting one to observe, and the author also noticed that it is always the least competent leaders who tend to deny past mistakes or to attribute them to their associates, predecessors or incompetent advisors. Few were able to face their investors and financial analysts to explain what happened and the reasons underlying the decisions that were taken during the 2008 crisis. And there was no need to go into technical or confidential details for this. This attitude is faulty. The market increasingly recognises that success boils down to leadership quality and the institution's strategic market position. An executive who has the humility and courage to face his or her failures shows through this acknowledgement that he or she masters the process. The executive will be better equipped to guide his or her business through recovery, a reflection that stems from observing numerous executives across a multitude of groups. A former executive, managing director of an investment bank which lost billions was dismissed when he had absolute authority over his bank. When he left, he managed not only to avoid taxes on the several million bonus that he was granted for his docility in answering to the press and to the public sector. Yet he now tells all who would listen that he was deceived by his associate, his teams, even though he used to terrorise them and that the most disastrous of investments were those that were made in violation of internal rules of his own banks' risk division. This example, less known to the public but bearing the hallmark of many other situations brings up the question of sanctions in our democracies. In this sense, to provide the regulator with the power to grant and withdraw banking licenses to banking executives is a good idea, if one knows how to build a simple and reasonable legal framework for their withdrawal (a public intervention should automatically trigger an inquiry of a licence withdrawal procedure).

Pride, greed, carelessness, selfishness, incompetence

Pride, greed, carelessness, selfishness, incompetence: the list seems a bit too generic and overwhelming to correspond to real life. However, these ingredients were almost systematically observed by the author in all institutions that were swept away by the 2008 crisis. The weighting of each factor varied depending on the institution and some countries - mainly Ireland and Spain, and Greece in another manner - the evolution of the macroeconomic environment led to a dilution of human accountability. They are nevertheless everywhere. It was impossible to recover within a reasonable amount of time reliable figures for a Greek bank. It was impossible to challenge a Spanish or Irish bank's executive management with regards to its direct or indirect exposure to the real estate bubble[71].

Many European bank executives had built themselves a luxurious ivory tower, with secretaries to screen visitors, drivers and other lifestyle artifices … No discussion addressing key issues was possible as they had to cut short meetings due to the string of meetings that they needed to tend to. This gave them the illusion of their own importance and of their control over their balance sheet. Both herd mentality and an extremely accommodating economic climate comforts executives in their blindness. These have not assumed their role as leaders, looking in the long-term. The following extract is an obvious case:

« "A ten-years outlook: … With the excellent vision of future markets, Dexia is confident in its ability to deliver on a standalone basis, average annual growth earnings of around 10%" - 2007 Annual Report (whereas the crisis had already begun).

In actual fact, the lack of clear-cut and thorough delegation accentuates the teams' lack of accountability and adds to the increased isolation of senior executive management. This blinded executives into a state not unlike that of drunkenness, flattered their ego and thus moved them away from the humility necessary for a long-term vision. The media got involved. Bonuses and markets were high and the entire system got overly excited: the slightest Landesbank, European medium-sized bank, perceived itself as a competitor of the big Wall Street firms and gave itself the same profitability goals, while at the same time they did not really understand the investment banking business or could not assume the risks of the business. Yet this pressure for results pushed them to take on more risk, to generate NBI (without any cost when they were buying packaged assets) to the point of making errors of judgment on the underlying fundamental risk. It is

---

[71] A little anecdote: I tried in 2009 to challenge the president and the CEO of a major Spanish bank on their exposure. We already knew at the time that the Spanish real estate market had to be corrected by 50%. The president repeatedly explained that the manner concerned only the Cajas, and at the end of the meeting, turning to my CEO, he smiled and tapped me amicably on the shoulder while laughing "very bright but very tough " he said… At least he knew the reality.

interesting to note that risk management procedures have not been respected in most cases. The author remembers two absolutely symmetrical conversations that he had in two institutions in different countries, but where the level of loss is counted in billions of euros.

The first conversation took place shortly after the institution's bail-out. I was trying to map the risks that led to the disaster with the former Chief Risk Officer of the institution, a responsible man, a man with integrity, still bruised by the bitter failure of the bank collapse and lack of support from his superiors. He had been difficult to approach, expecting to be yet again morally crucified by the arrival of the bail-out team sent by the state to clean up the situation. He was surprised and then was gradually appeased by our approach, which consisted more of compassion and curiosity than judgment. Damage was done, the past was the past and we were focused on the future: protecting public assets and restoring the situation. As it turned out, 99% of the bank was healthy and useful to the economy. The former Chief Risk Officer felt increasingly valued as we worked together. He took it to heart to work with us in great transparency, relieved of such unexpected support which ultimately helped him regain his self-esteem and his self-confidence. We quickly realized that he was competent, and therefore he was precious to us. We worked this way for several weeks and one winter evening, as he was at ease, as the darkness had set outside the office and contributed to this atmosphere of trust, likely to lead us to the truth, I asked him a critical question: "But how could the bank have validated such a level of investment in ABSs CDO lines (the most famous toxic product of the 2008 crisis?". The answer was spontaneous, immediate, "But Serge, we have not validated any. Each bond acquisition was directly signed by the CEO, outside the delegation of the risk committee. We even wrote that we had some reservations." Everything was said.

The second conversation took place later in another country and another institution, as teams had been changed and bank fire's burning embers had cooled down. The Chief Risk Officer was still visibly bruised by his dismissal and the feeling of injustice related to the situation: his CEO had left in very good financial conditions without ever losing his luster or his arrogance whereas his own career was broken. The conversation was interesting. The bankers sought to explain to me what Risks Committees were for: "He (the general manager) terrorized everyone, asserted his authority with fire and often threatened his associates in public with the following type of statements "if you are not able to take such risks, we will find someone who can". He cut expenses down without thinking, in a primal way: "how many are you? Ten? I want two out by the end of the quarter ... " The worst was regarding risk-taking: if we recommend exposure at EUR 300mn, he would accuse us of being meek, not wanting to grow his bank, wanting to play in the second category, that it was necessary to generate income and often he would triple the exposure. All ABS lines were taken under his pressure. He had gradually isolated the most conservative executives or replaced them with obliging courtiers who were there to carry out his orders". *The example is particularly typical as it was common knowledge that the CEO was incompetent to lead an investment bank, had inadequate training, had no professional experience in CIB, had non-existent international work experience, his knowledge of English was poor yet the system carried him to this leadership position. His temper just as his greed were known. Yet to my knowledge, the board had not expressed any reservations with regards to his appointment.*

Of the many conversations that the author had with executives of troubled institutions, few have acknowledged that they had made mistakes. The few who did turned out to be competent and generally from posts external to general management. Systematically, institutions have been dysfunctional at senior management level due to human errors which too often may be qualified as the consequence of psychological disorders. Management was not working as a team, executive officers did not trust each other...

From a human point of view, these situations have generated little courageous behavior of outright opposition, which is quite logical. And when some executives, often in risk departments, but also at the front, raised their voices against excessive leverage or excessive risk-taking, they have been systematically excluded. Moreover, all banks were leveraging massively their balance sheets and no risk did crystalize, therefore these professionals had a very fragile position and were routinely described as Cassandras. We must recognize that often it is those who were more cautious in nature who were first to express reservations. They were therefore already qualified as such in collective consensus and their position was found to be less credible. This concrete psychological process shows that unfortunately the problem was elsewhere: only much stricter definitions of risk limits and of the development strategy would have avoided these excesses, which unfortunately are all too human.

Harmony, confidence and competence

Conversely, the teams that best addressed the crisis had known each other for a long time, trusted each other, respected their CEO and their Chairman and supported their decisions.

I remember a trip in the Thalis while I was sitting next to the BNPP team management. The CEO of the time (B. Prost) was explaining to his associate (J.L. Bonnafé) and his team something regarding the organization. He was practical, to the point. The conversation was animated and lively, with a clear objective, the various opportunities and challenges had been addressed and discussed. It is clear that the four men could work together, respected each other and were skilled. This harmony in the working method, respect for the hierarchy, and adherence to goals were even more evident in the negotiations with the government. Teams often tended to be harsh, almost rigid in discussions, trying to push the advantage of the bank to its maximum, at the risk of irritating the Belgian Government until an arbitration from management would cool down the situation, generally decisions were reasonable and based on common sense. Their position was then accordingly adjusted immediately to the new instruction. The way they functioned was so obvious that following two to three rounds of negotiation, government negotiators adjusted their approach accordingly. They then were satisfied with a process of simply identifying excesses and bringing those up with top management. (The BNPP method in my perspective nevertheless presents the disadvantage of not empowering teams enough. Making management aware of disagreements would be more efficient if it was first done internally. However, perhaps this was already the case and teams simply did not want to signal that there was a possibility of negotiation at first, or maybe they were just acting accordingly to the instruction of their hierarchy).

Withstanding the pressure

The last point of moral courage that the crisis highlighted is the executives' ability to weather the storm by keeping a cool head. A number of very arrogant bankers, and even contemptuous of their central bankers completely panicked when they saw their liquidity dry up. Nowadays this weakness is of course already forgotten and with it were forgotten the good resolutions of reducing liquidity transformation, a strategy that only the umbrella of the central bank makes possible. Yet many central bankers can testify that they saw bank executive management totally panic when focus should have been on action and firm as well as responsible decisions. They were still stuck in their inability to assume losses and just had the reflex of reverting to state authority when the situation started to become complex. This attitude raises the question of the added value of such executive management which is obviously only able to manage day-to-day business. Doing quite the opposite, other executive managements have really recognised the precariousness of their situation and have taken firm action to adjust their balance sheet accordingly. In doing so they favored the survival of their institution. Such institutions generally had a strong and respected CFO, who was able to impose in particular to the trading rooms decisions to cut off liquidity and increase its price.

For the reader to get a sense of the panic that the crisis induced in some executives, I will give only one example. I was at the office of an executive whose institution had been put under the central bank's infusion. Had it not, it clearly would have literally collapsed, carrying into the wreck millions of savers and businesses. The man was leaning his elbows on his desk, holding his head in his hands and he kept saying that we had a foreign exchange risk issue (on dollar assets funded in euros). This was true, but relative to credit losses that would irreparably devour the financial institution's own capital funds, the issue that he focused on was minor and technically manageable. Four years later, this executive was back in a top managerial position under the spotlight of the media and fortunately seems to have forgotten the incident (which was embarrassing to witness for the author) and is back again (unfortunately perhaps) in his full superb.

A regulator (foreign) referred to a telephone conversation with the executive management of one of the largest institutions in the world screaming on the phone obviously totally panicked and distraught. At least, they recognized the gravity of the situation and their inability to cope on their own.

On the other side of the spectrum, many banks faced the storm with calmness and lucidity. In France, despite the high losses collected between the ABSs and the Greek crisis, particularly observed with the key cooperative banks, banks have managed overcome the peak of the liquidity crisis. They managed to gradually readjust their liquidity model, with both firmness and consistency. The long-term consequence on their business model is still being debated, except for the case of BNPP.

CONCLUSION: MAINTAIN LONG-TERM VISION

By modeling the bank over the long-term, we move away from the short-term vision unsuited to a profession where the instantaneous probability of client default increases generally over time as margins remain equal throughout the duration of a loan. Through this approach we gain greater insights into the consequences of own's decisions in terms of capital funds and liquidity. It follows that, except in very specific cases of market anomaly, one must not grow too fast. In banks, customers are difficult to acquire on balanced tariffs. The relationship is built over time and customer transfers are slow: there is no easy money in the long-term nor is there technical superiority of a structural nature. Competition is too intense for technical advantage not to be quickly copied by competitors. Nor is the market dominated by an inefficient historic actor from which a newcomer could quickly take over market share. E-banks and their reduced cost structure are not able to place themselves fast enough as leading players to take over a significant market share of traditional networks: these are gradually adapting their networks, close branches, create their own websites and call platforms. They are gradually transferring their customers to the new available structure while concurrently reducing banking costs.

In this context, the density of the industry at the national level does not seem to be an issue of a structural nature. For proof, operating ratios of many smaller-sized banks are lower than those of larger banks. And when we look at the IT budgets of some groups, there is still potential for economies of scale and industrialization. The contribution of new technologies has not fully penetrated the major banking networks, which still have much work to clean up and update their databases, and optimise their IT management.

However, the concentration cycle at the European level has not really started. It alone would allow for the real diversification of country risk. The creation of European supervision in this regard is a rare phenomenon where the regulator is in anticipation of the market. Also, mergers which we should see come into effect in the coming years will be either cross-border, or they will have the objective of strengthening the domestic market share of an actor with European ambition, wanting to build on a solid local base to launch its European development. In both cases, the regulator will encourage the process and probably more and more governments will graciously host an international giant that is in a position to stabilize their market and to prevent the unforeseeable tax issues that we have seen over the recent years.

The other major trend that is not even being discussed is the integration of national cooperative banks in European cooperative networks much alike current systems of mutual networks supervised by a national head of cooperative networks, itself owned by the regional banks that it supervises (Rabobank, Crédit Agricole…). This trend is the only solution for a sector that cannot otherwise quickly raise equity in the case of difficulties: no cooperative bank has managed to expand internationally or outside its core business, except for a few cases which are often at the limit of their capabilities. These difficulties are in fact structural to the core of a system that is based on proximity. Mutualists must choose between abandoning their model and thus ensuing demutualization or reaffirming of their mutual value. The first solution (demutualization) opens up the possibility of international development and facilitates raising capital, but it also implies the risk of the potential disappearance (as in England for many). The second solution shall require if mutualists want to survive the opening of their system to other cooperative banks beyond their borders. One day, a mutual network will measure the implications of this reflection and will launch a movement of cross-border alliances, which will fundamentally alter the existing banking landscape. This is perhaps a way for some to come out of the existential crisis in which changes in society threw them.

A competition that is increasingly European should add a more segmented competition. Banks are aware nowadays that the 20/80 rule applies particularly well to the sector with 20% of customers often generating the bulk of revenues. The competition is expected to increase on the most profitable market segment, which will push down margins and require a better analysis of income statements and pricing schemes.

Nevertheless a well-managed and sufficiently large traditional European bank is structurally profitable despite the current pressure on margins. Since the Roman Empire, the economy has relied on its banks to develop. Banks thus enjoy from a strategic point of view a healthy structural position and long-term profitability prospects. This raises the question of reinvestment (or distribution) of incomes generated each year by banking core businesses: growth across borders, repositioning in other niches (insurance, personal services …). Nowadays, no group has really become a balanced major insurer/banker or a banking/trading group ... The subject remains open with regards to reinvestment of the generated banking incomes to other parts of the economy or of the choice of their full distribution to shareholders if they are no longer needed for banking.

Finance remains a sector of the future and the coming years will be rich in reflections, transformations and opportunities.

BIBLIOGRAPHY

Abrahams, S. (2006). *Quick guide to agency mortgage backed securities*. Bear Stearns.

Armatte, M. et al. (1988). *Estimation et sondages, cinq contributions à l'histoire de la statistique*. Economica.

Basel Committee on Banking Supervision. (2004). *Principles for the Management and Supervision of Interest Rate Risk* [Internet]. Bank for International Settlements, Basel. Available from: <http://www.bis.org/publ/bcbs108.pdf> [accessed 2016].

Basel Committee on Banking Supervision. (2006). *International Convergence of Capital Measurement and Capital Standards, A Revised Framework Comprehensive Version* [Internet]. Bank for International Settlements, Basel. Available from: <http://www.bis.org/publ/bcbs128.pdf> [accessed 2016].

Basel Committee on Banking Supervision. (2008). *Principles for Sound Liquidity Risk Monitoring and Supervision* [Internet]. Bank for International Settlements, Basel. Available from: <http://www.bis.org/publ/bcbs144.pdf> [accessed 2016].

Basel Committee on Banking Supervision. (2009). *Enhancements to the Basel II framework* [Internet]. Bank for International Settlements, Basel. Available from: <http://www.bis.org/publ/bcbs157.pdf> [accessed 2016].

Basel Committee on Banking Supervision. (2011). *Basel III: A global regulatory framework for more resilient banks and banking systems* [Internet]. Bank for International Settlements, Basel. Available from: <http://www.bis.org/publ/bcbs189.pdf> [accessed 2016].

Basel Committee on Banking Supervision. (2013). *Basel III: The Liquidity Coverage Ratio and liquidity risk monitoring tools* [Internet]. Bank for International Settlements, Basel. Available from: <http://www.bis.org/publ/bcbs238.pdf> [accessed 2016].

Blanchard, O. et al. (2010). *Rethinking Macroeconomic Policy* [Internet]. IMF Staff Position Note SPN/10/03, 12 February 2010, http://www.imf.org/external/pubs/ft/spn/2010/spn1003.pdf [accessed 2016].

Eggertsson, G.B. and Paul Krugman. (2010). *Debt, deleveraging and the liquidity trap: a Fisher-Minsky-Koo approach*.

Étude du Rapport annuel de la Commission bancaire - 2006. (2006). Banque de France, Place of Publication. Available from: <www.banque-france.fr/fileadmin/user_upload/banque_de_france/archipel/publications/cb_ra/etudes_cb_ra/cb_ra_2006_02.pdf> [accessed 2016].

European Central Bank. (2015). *Collateral* [Internet] : <http://www.ecb.europa.eu/paym/coll/html/index.en.html> [accessed 2016].

Eurostat. (2014). Manual on Government Deficit and Debt: implementation of ESA 2010, 2014 edition, pp.431: <http://ec.europa.eu/eurostat/documents/3859598/5937189/KS-GQ-14-010-EN.PDF/> [accessed 2016]

Frachot, A. and C. Gourieroux. (1993). *Titrisation et remboursements anticipés.* ENSAE.

Frachot, A. et al. (2003). Méthodologie de gestion actif/passif. *Economica.*

Réglement CRBF 97-02 relatif au contrôle interne www.banque-france.fr/cclrf/fr/pdf/CRBF97_02.pdf

Arrêté du 20 février 2007 de transposition de la directive Européenne sur Bâle II : http://www.banque-france.fr/cclrf/fr/pdf/20070220arr_arr_29_10_09.pdf

Kälberer, W. et al. (ed.) (2015). *2015 ECBC European Covered Bond Fact Book 10th edition* [Internet]. European Mortgage Federation - European Covered Bond Council (EMF-ECBC), Brussels. Available from: <http://intranet.hypo.org/docs/1/JFOHGCODFCGLPBBPCBKNHPMBPDWK9DBDGYTE4Q/EMF/Docs/DLS/2014-00041.pdf> [accessed 2016].

Kramer, B. and Gyan Sinha. (2006). *Quick guide to non-agency mortgage backed securities.* Bear Stearns.

La crise de la dette souveraine. (2012). *Documents et débats*, No.4, May. Banque de France, place of publication. Available from: <http://www.banque-france.fr/fileadmin/user_upload/banque_de_france/publications/Documents_Economiques/documents-et-debats-numero-4-integral.pdf>.

Moulin, S. (2012). *Notions de mathématiques financières.* ALM-Vision.

Moulin, S. (2008). Banks die by liquidity bleeding, Bear Stearns Research Papers.

Verband Deutscher PfandbriefBanken website www.pfandbrief.org

Tilman, L. (ed.) (2003). *Asset/Liability Management of Financial Institutions, Maximizing shareholder value through risk-conscious investing.* Bear Stearns / Institutional Investor Books.